Project-Based Writing in Science

Bold Visions in Educational Research
Volume 41

Scope:
Bold Visions in Educational Research is international in scope and includes books from two areas: *teaching and learning to teach* and *research methods in education*. Each area contains multi-authored handbooks of approximately 200,000 words and monographs (authored and edited collections) of approximately 130,000 words. All books are scholarly, written to engage specified readers and catalyze changes in policies and practices. Defining characteristics of books in the series are their explicit uses of theory and associated methodologies to address important problems. We invite books from across a theoretical and methodological spectrum from scholars employing quantitative, statistical, experimental, ethnographic, semiotic, hermeneutic, historical, ethnomethodological, phenomenological, case studies, action, cultural studies, content analysis, rhetorical, deconstructive, critical, literary, aesthetic and other research methods.

Books on *teaching and learning to teach* focus on any of the curriculum areas (e.g., literacy, science, mathematics, social science), in and out of school settings, and points along the age continuum (pre K to adult). The purpose of books on *research methods in education* is **not** to present generalized and abstract procedures but to show how research is undertaken, highlighting the particulars that pertain to a study. Each book brings to the foreground those details that must be considered at every step on the way to doing a good study. The goal is **not** to show how generalizable methods are but to present rich descriptions to show how research is enacted. The books focus on methodology, within a context of substantive results so that methods, theory, and the processes leading to empirical analyses and outcomes are juxtaposed. In this way method is not reified, but is explored within well-described contexts and the emergent research outcomes. Three illustrative examples of books are those that allow proponents of particular perspectives to interact and debate, comprehensive handbooks where leading scholars explore particular genres of inquiry in detail, and introductory texts to particular educational research methods/issues of interest to novice researchers.

Project-Based Writing in Science

Lawrence Baines
The University of Oklahoma

SENSE PUBLISHERS
ROTTERDAM/BOSTON/TAIPEI

A C.I.P. record for this book is available from the Library of Congress.

ISBN: 978-94-6209-669-1 (paperback)
ISBN: 978-94-6209-670-7 (hardback)
ISBN: 978-94-6209-671-4 (e-book)

Published by: Sense Publishers,
P.O. Box 21858,
3001 AW Rotterdam,
The Netherlands
https://www.sensepublishers.com/

Printed on acid-free paper

To mom, as always

Special thanks to Melanie and Anastasia for helping with the research.

TABLE OF CONTENTS

LIST OF FIGURES

FOREWORD TO LAWRENCE BAINES'
PROJECT-BASED WRITING IN SCIENCE

BY DR. MICHAEL L. BENTLEY

"If you cannot – in the long run – tell someone what you have been doing, your doing has been worthless." - Nobel Laureate Edwin Schrodinger (1951)

As a science teacher or teacher educator, you will find this a very engaging book. The first thing that came to my mind when I read it was how I would use it in my courses in elementary and secondary science teaching methods. In fact, I used a few things from the book right away, sharing with my students Chapter One's of eight essential science websites, as well as the possible writing assignments that were itemized and the "Listener Out-of-Class" worksheet. The latter accompanies Lawrence Baines' suggestion about the value of students sharing their work with people other than their teachers. After the student reads to him or her, that selected listener, or "LOC," writes down the student's responses to a few questions about the piece, and gives it back to the student to submit as his or her homework assignment. Addressing an outside audience lets the student explain one or more science concepts to someone else, and thereby develop his or her own understanding. In addition, the child's teacher escapes some of the dreaded chore of grading and gets valuable free help in providing formative assessment.

For anyone like myself who is regularly engaged in teacher preparation and credentialing and professional development courses, this book presents a well-researched argument for why writing should be emphasized as a key teaching method in science education at all levels. In addition to providing a substantial rationale for the pedagogy, Baines provides a set of five examples in different science disciplines that demonstrate specifically how writing can be used to make instruction more effective at the classroom lesson level. Better yet, these lessons represent "best practices" in science teaching because they all incorporate inquiry and active learning strategies. And certainly the various levels of writing tasks suggested in the sample lessons are all "minds-on" strategies.

This is a book that John Dewey would very much appreciate. Dewey is associated with the idea that 'we learn by doing' but his position perhaps is confused with the Chinese saying, 'I do, and I understand.' But what Dewey actually wrote was, "Give the pupils something to do, not something to learn; and the doing is of such a nature as to demand thinking; learning naturally results." So, what Dewey really means is that we learn by *thinking*. And Lawrence Baines shares with fellow educators a number of strategies to get kids to think more deeply (through writing) about the science content of the classroom curriculum. Few students will be able to resist being engaged with the real-life scenarios and fascinating science in the sample lessons. Most of the lessons could be adapted for classroom use in upper elementary, middle and high school, and even college science classes. They are also great examples of integrating science and language arts in the classroom curriculum that teacher educators like me can use in undergraduate and graduate science methods courses and in professional development workshops.

Chapter 1 in this book describes three levels of student writing, a useful categorization for making assignments and helpful in assessing student work. The "quickwrite" is completed by students in a few minutes and represents a level one writing assignment. Baines states, "The purpose of a quickwrite may be to give students the opportunity to capture their thoughts at a particular moment in time and put them into words. Without the time to reflect, scientific concepts can quickly turn into confused notions…"

The quickwrite exercise helps students focus and reflect on the content but is usually not graded. It is also is a way for the teacher to guide student thinking in a desired direction. The next level writing assignment, level two, falls between this and a research-type paper, or term paper, which represents the level three writing assignment. As Baines notes, most writing in the science classroom is to inform or persuade a specific audience, and all requires some degree of reflection on the facts and concepts of the lesson. The level 3 is the most demanding work and usually a more long-term project.

In Chapter 2 Baines shares a number of valuable ways teachers can reduce the time normally spent grading papers, tips that most teachers will find especially helpful. He describes one teacher who only gives grades of zero or A to students on their writing assignments. While this may sound harsh, the teacher has found that students have responded well to the challenge and he has few failures. The secret strategy is how he enables students to get help from peers and other adults. From assessing student writing, a teacher can quickly grasp where comprehension is solid and where it breaks down. In this chapter Baines recommends teachers share scoring rubrics for assignments with students so that the grading criteria are up front. As one who uses rubrics in teaching, I can testify that they are very helpful in both guiding students in their work and in later justifying an evaluation to the student and to others if necessary, such as instructional supervisors and parents during parent-teacher conferences. Finally in Chapter 2, Baines discusses the National Assessment of Educational Progress and the criteria for evaluating writing used in its prestigious national assessments, criteria that can be used by science teachers in assessing student writing.

In his earlier book, *A teacher's guide to multisensory learning*, Baines (2008) wrote about the value of simulations in teaching and learning. In terms of impact, he claims that learning through simulations and models is second only to direct, physical experience, and I concur. In fact, medical training, pilot training, and military training are all dependent upon realistic simulations of what the learner will likely encounter in his or her professional practice. In Chapters 3 to 7 Baines provides sample lessons in which the main context of learning is often a realistic and engaging simulation.

The five chapters representing model lessons are well organized and go right to the point for quick access. In each Baines provides a description of the activity, relevant research, anchor points and a challenge to focus the study, a timeline, concise objectives, a summary of the lesson, required materials, a list of essential websites, how to set up the lesson, a detailed but succinct procedure indicating where writing activities occur in the sequence, clarifying comments, ideas for enrichment activities, annotated references, and finally, recommendations for assessment. Many of the lessons also include useful reproducible handouts and worksheets.

In Chapter 3, 'Going Viral,' Baines first presents a number of dramatic facts about viruses that are bound to capture student imagination. He follows with a lesson scenario in which the World Health Organization (WHO) asks for help in preventing a pandemic of the bird flu. Students soak up a lot of the biology of cells in the role-play as they create an action plan that will prevent a pandemic. In this chapter Baines refers to several of my favorite books that featured viruses threatening human populations: Stephen King's *The Stand*, Robin Cook's *Contagion* (about Ebola Hemorrhagic Fever), Michael Crichton's *Andromeda Strain*, and Richard Preston's *The Hot Zone*, real-life bio-thriller about a mutated form of Ebola called Reston virus (RESTV) discovered in Reston, Virginia in the early 1990s, less than 24 km. from Washington, DC. These Biosafety Level 4 agents are so dangerous to humans because they are highly infectious, have a high death rate, and have no known cures. Working on this simulation will likely lead students to become interested in infectious diseases and especially these exotic tropical diseases. No doubt many will delve into these chilling fictional and non-fiction books.

Chapter 4 is titled, 'Survival of the Smartest.' Here Baines structures an inquiry lesson around a survival simulation that actually taps into the *U.S. Army Survival Manual*. He argues that if students learn about real risks associated with environments like deserts and conditions like hypothermia and how they could survive themselves when exposed to hazardous situations, they will use their higher order reasoning skills to propose possible solutions in the role-play. The six different survival situations presented in the chapter will challenge students with multiple problems and complications. Thinking through all the options will require them to analyze, synthesize, and evaluate how they might survive. This is truly a simulation that could pay off for some of them in the future!

Chapter 5 is about the physics of running and while not based upon a simulation activity, students will find this study very engaging too (because it is about themselves) – and may even lead to improving their health and performance. Most students like and follow sports and the exercises in this chapter provides them with basic knowledge of the laws of motion as well as how to measure relevant bodily parameters related to speed, velocity, displacement, distance, and friction. As Herman (2008) notes, "Physics explains everything from the beginning to the end of any complete description of the human body" (p. vii). Completing the worksheets provided at the end of the chapter require team/group work in the out of doors and focus on measuring, recording, graphing and interpreting results.

In Chapter 6, The Fight for Water, Baines addresses a global environmental problem that particularly affects communities in the Western United States which depends on groundwater from the vast Ogallala Aquifer, which lies under 453,000 square kilometers in Kansas, Nebraska, South Dakota, Colorado, Oklahoma, Texas, Wyoming and New Mexico and yields 30 percent of the nation's irrigated groundwater. This fossil water, left over from the melting of the last continental glaciers 11,000 years ago, is rapidly being drawn down. In fact, in 2011 Kansas alone pumped out 1.3 trillion gallons, more than enough to fill Lake Okeechobee in Florida! Geologists estimate that if the drawdown stops now, it would still take about a thousand years to replenish it. They predict that at current rates of extraction it will be 70 percent gone by 2060.

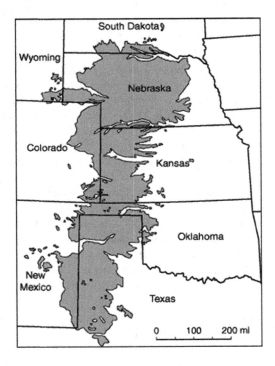

Actually, few people really grasp how little fresh water is available to us. Surface water, found in rivers and lakes, makes up only 1% of all fresh water and many people around the world lack access to it. For this simulation, students are challenged to deal with water management for the city of Las Vegas, Nevada, whose source is the Colorado River reservoir at Lake Mead. Water levels there have fallen steadily for nearly a decade and so water is one of the most politically charged local issues, and certainly one of the most important. In this simulation students have to analyze water usage and devise a 10-year plan for the city's water. Students have to consider geography, public policy, individual rights, and governmental authority versus private property rights. In drawing up a plan they learn about population growth and the increasing demand for water, the different sources and uses of water in a city, and the costs involved in providing potable water from sources far away.

The final chapter, 'It's a Dog's Life.' is one of my favorites, and I have to confess that I shared several ideas about multimedia assignments from this chapter with my pre-service teacher education class. The science is about classification and requires students to observe and document, research, analyze, and categorize animals and plants that they find at home or in their neighborhood environment. The product of the study is a descriptive photo essay that ranks as a level 3 research paper. The medium will intrigue students and most will love sharing information about their pets and the plants and associated critters where they live.

In concluding, I want to mention that in Chapter 1 Baines cites Jared Diamond's Pulitzer-prize-winning book *Guns, Germs, and Steel* (1997) as an example of a well-researched attempt to persuade. Diamond posits that environmental factors may account for the decline and failure of one culture and the flourishing of another, rather than cultural factors, like intelligence or work ethic. I found this to be a fascinating treatise and so was his follow-up, *Collapse: How Societies Choose to Fail or Succeed* (2011), in which he argues that environmental issues are often the main catalyst for decline, especially when combined with a society's disregard for what is happening. Diamond, I think, wants us to be aware of these past societal experiences, so we will avoid potential devastations to come. *Collapse* is a compelling read and global climate change looms, in my opinion, as one of the greatest challenges facing humanity (and all the other species on the Earth as well). I believe the kind of science teaching exemplified in Lawrence Baines' *Project-Based Writing in Science* is part of the solution: educating our students to think and act in effective ways to survive and preserve our precious planet.

REFERENCES

Baines, L. (2008). *A teacher's guide to multisensory learning: Improving literacy by engaging the senses.* Alexandria, VA: Association for Supervision and Curriculum Development.

Diamond, J. (2011). Collapse: *How Societies Choose to Fail or Succeed*, Revised Ed. New York: Penguin Books.

PROJECT-BASED WRITING IN SCIENCE

It is incredible to consider that writing has not always been an integral part of the science curriculum. After all, the world's greatest scientists are known as much for what they wrote as what they contributed to science. It would be difficult to separate Charles Darwin from *The Origin of Species*, Isaac Newton from *Principia Mathematica*, Nicolaus Copernicus from *On the Revolutions of Heavenly Spheres*, E. O. Wilson from *On Human Nature*, Albert Einstein from "On the Electrodynamics of Moving Bodies," or James D. Watson from *The Double Helix*.

Indeed, book bestseller lists commonly feature works by scientists, such as Primo Levi, Brian Green, Michio Kaku, Richard Dawkins, and Oliver Sacks. Novelist Michael Crichton was an MD and graduate of Harvard Medical School; prolific science fiction writer Isaac Asimov was a professor of biochemistry at Boston University who also happened to write books, more than 500 of them. The interplay between writing and scientific advancement has a long, illustrious history.

According to the National Research Council, about half of the time spent by scientists and engineers is spent reading and writing (2011). Thus, writing not only helps students learn, but writing also has the advantage of helping to develop skills that will prove useful for students in "life after high school." The College Board (2004) classifies writing as a "threshold skill," meaning that the ability to write serves as a gateway, or threshold, to more intellectually-demanding, more responsible, higher-paying jobs. In a survey of 120 American companies, writing was cited as one of the most indispensible skills that a prospective employee could possess (College Board, 2004). The survey also revealed that:

- Two-thirds of salaried employees in large American companies have some writing responsibility.
- Eighty percent or more of the companies with the greatest employment growth potential, assess writing during hiring.
- More than half of all responding companies report that they "frequently" or "almost always" produce technical reports (59 percent), formal reports (62 percent), and memos and correspondence (70 percent). (pp. 3-4)

Today, the centrality of writing in science is acknowledged in the New Generation Science Standards (2013), with its emphasis on "cross-cutting concepts," "planning and conducting investigations," and "communicating scientific and technical information" (pp. 33-39; 65-73). Reports from the Organization of Economic Cooperation and Development (OECD, 2012) confirm the centrality of science and innovative thinking to the quality of life across the globe.

The Common Core State Standards (CCSS) Initiative in the United States, which pledges to make all students "college and career ready," insists that students must be "prepared to read, write, and research across the curriculum, including in history and science" (2013). Writing is "essential to the economic success of the nation," according to a 2010 report from NAEP, the National Assessment of Educational Progress (p. 1).

However, the importance of writing in science goes beyond the directives of the CCSS, New Generation Science Standards, and the NAEP. Perhaps the strongest proof of the importance of writing in science is the multitude of journals, newspapers, newsletters, blogs, and websites dedicated to communicating the latest, greatest breakthroughs. Judging from the popularity of science websites, writing in science has a massive and expanding fan base. Some useful science websites are as follows:

Although it is not yet in the top ten of most popular websites, WolframAlpha is a massive search engine for mathematics and science that is being utilized in educational settings throughout the world. A beta site, expressly for educators, which contains lessons, demonstrations, and online articles and books is located at http://education.wolfram.com.

When J. Craig Venter's team developed the first "synthetic life," an artificial version of the bacterium Mycoplasma mycoides in May 2010, headlines proclaiming the event could be found on websites and newspapers throughout the world, including *The New York Times*. In fact, a search on The *New York Times* database reveals more than seventy articles on J. Craig Venter.

Figure 1. Essential science websites

Organization and website address	Unique visitors per month	Focus of the website
National Oceanic and Atmospheric Administration (NOAA) www.noaa.gov	10 million	The website states, "From daily weather forecasts, severe storm warnings and climate monitoring to fisheries management, coastal restoration and supporting marine commerce, NOAA's products and services support economic vitality and affect more than one-third of America's gross domestic product."
National Aeronautics and Space Administration (NASA) www.nasa.gov	9 million	The site features large, "for educators" sections, designated by grade level, from kindergarten to higher education.
Science Direct www.Sciencedirect.com	4.5 million	The site serves as a clearing house of sorts for scientific journals and includes a list of "hottest 25 articles" by area of interest.
Science Daily www.sciencedaily.com	2.4 million	The site features daily breaking news, summaries of important articles in academic journals, and recent scientific discoveries.
Nature www.nature.com	1.8 million	One of the most respected weekly, international science journal in the world.
Popular Science www.popsci.com	1.4 million	Despite the irritating ads, this website sometimes features highly engaging articles told in everyday language.
New Scientist www.newscientist.com	1 million	Features interesting stories on a variety of topics, including the environment, health, physics/math, and science in society
Live Science www.livescience.com	Almost 1 million	Features image galleries, collections of infographics, and "coolest science stories of the week."

(Estimate for unique visitors per month from Ebizmba, 2013)

Indeed, the rate of change in science is one reason that the field is so exciting. It is impossible for even the most contemporary e-textbook to capture the current state of science or to anticipate all of the disruptive discoveries on the horizon. Thus, although most recently published science textbooks are beautifully-constructed and well-organized, when considering the latest developments in science, a teacher may want to supplement the textbook with outside resources. Articles, images, and video from most science websites are open access and can be used freely by teachers for face-to-face, classroom instruction.

THE POWER OF WRITING

Writing is a convenient way to record observations, crystalize thinking, gain an understanding of scientific concepts, and contemplate the vast world of possibilities.

"In an era in which many of the borders that have long separated the world's peoples blur, exploring and sharing human experience through writing helps define not only individual identity but also the universal connections that people share" (National Assessment of Educational Progress, 2010, p. 3).

However, simply assigning more writing will not magically transform students into highly-engaged, eloquent, scholars of science. Writing assignments must be strategic, purposeful, and—perhaps most important of all—interesting. When making an initial writing assignment, an effective strategy is to focus on the conceptual big picture before delving into the gory details and sophisticated nomenclature endemic to specialized areas of study. Once students understand the basic concepts, then details are more likely to stick.

About the importance of piquing student interest, Farr (2013) writes:

A thoroughly researched conclusion about learning is that students will put in the time and energy necessary to learn if they are interested in what they are learning and if they can relate to it. (p. 2)

Making attractive entry points for writing is well worth the effort. Linking material to current news stories or events is one way to garner student interest. As well, there is no shortage of modern-day, science-related challenges that could serve as compelling entry points—species extinction, bio-engineered food, the ethics of nanotechnological engineering, pollution, population density, natural resource depletion, water, energy supply, the list seems endless. Learning about these challenges in the context of science and the realities of modern life can provide powerful incentives for writing.

WRITING AND STANDARDS

Perhaps the table that has appeared most often on school district memoranda concerning the Common Core in the United States is the chart explicating the desired ratio between fiction and nonfiction texts over time.

Figure 2. Ratio of reading literary vs. informational texts, suggested by Common Core

	Grade 4	Grade 8	Grade 12
Literary texts	50	45	30
Informational texts	50	55	70

The basic point of the table is that, over time, students should have ever-expanding opportunities to read nonfiction texts in all of their classes. Of course, the logical next step after reading a variety of nonfiction texts is to have students create nonfiction texts of their own. Indeed, the kind of reading that students are expected to do aligns with the kind of writing that students are expected to do.

Common Core State Standards emphasize unequivocally that persuasive and informative writing should take precedence over other kinds of writing:

> Evidence concerning the demands of college and career readiness gathered during development of the Standards concurs with NAEP's shifting emphases: standards for grades 9–12 describe writing in all three forms, but, consistent with NAEP, the overwhelming focus of writing throughout high school should be on arguments and informative/explanatory texts. (Common Core State Standards, 2013)

The writing prompts for the Common Core are based, to a large extent, upon long-established NAEP assessments. As indicated in Table 3 below, when the NAEP assesses writing, 80% of students will receive prompts that ask them to write an informative or persuasive essay, while only 20% will be asked to "convey experience." The inference is that the increase in persuasive and informative writing prompts should be reflected in a school's curriculum. In other words, as students get older, writing assignments should increasingly steer them towards persuasive and informative writing.

Figure 3. Writing prompts for the NAEP (2010)

	Grade 4	Grade 8	Grade 12
To persuade	30	35	40
To inform	35	35	40
To convey experience	35	30	20

INFORMATIVE WRITING

One of the most common forms of writing for scientists is the lab report, which attempts to capture accurate details and explicit results from experiments. The lab report is a classic, widely-acknowledged form of informative writing. The NAEP elaborates on the purposes of informative writing:

> Informative writing focuses primarily on the subject matter element in communication. This type of writing is used to share knowledge and to convey messages, instructions, and ideas. Like all writing, informative writing may be filtered through the writer's impressions, understanding, and feelings. Used as a means of exploration, informative writing helps both the writer and the reader to learn new ideas and to reexamine old conclusions. Informative writing may also involve reporting on events or experiences, or analyzing concepts and relationships, including developing hypotheses and generalizations. (National Association of Educational Progress, 2000, p. 3)

In addition to laboratory reports, any writing based upon observation and description may be categorized as informative. For example, asking students to investigate and communicate the habits, environment, and characteristics of a particular animal might make a good informative writing assignment (chapter 7). Describing how bacteria invade a cell, mutate, and replicate might serve as another topic for an informative piece of writing (chapter 3).

Explication, exposition, and *explanation* are terms that are often used interchangeably with *informative writing.* Although each term may have once possessed a distinctive connotation, in practice, *explication, exposition,* and *explanation* have become synonymous with *informative writing.*

PERSUASIVE WRITING

If you want to find an example of persuasive writing, you only have to peruse any grant application seeking funding support (money) from the National Science Foundation or the National Institutes of Health. The purpose of every grant application is to persuade an organization's review board that the proposed work is worthy of a significant influx of money. Guidelines for the NAEP Persuasive Writing Assessment are as follows.

> Persuasive writing focuses on the reader. Its primary aim is to influence others to take some action or bring about change. Persuasive writing may contain great amounts of information—facts, details, examples, comparisons, statistics, or anecdotes—but its main purpose is not simply to inform but to persuade. This type of writing involves a clear awareness of what arguments might most affect the audience being addressed. Writing persuasively also requires use of critical thinking skills such as analysis, inference, synthesis, and evaluation. Persuasive writing is called for in a variety of situations. It may involve making a response to a request for advice by giving an opinion and providing sound reasons to support it. It may also involve presenting an argument in a way that a particular audience will find convincing. When there is opposition, persuasive writing may entail refuting arguments that are contrary to the writer's point of view. (National Assessment of Educational Progress, 2010, p. 5)

Persuasive writing offers teachers rich opportunities to promote critical thinking, research, and presentation skills. A persuasive writing assignment might ask students to consider the problem of water scarcity in a particular region and to devise a plan to address the scarcity problem by providing a well-supported, detailed plan of action (chapter 6).

Jared Diamond's Pulitzer-prize-winning book *Guns, Germs, and Steel* (1997) is a detailed, well-researched, attempt to persuade. Diamond's thesis is that the reason one culture flourishes while another culture declines may be due to environmental factors, such as geography, climate, and access to natural resources—not cultural factors, such as ingenuity or work ethic. Diamond lays out his theory by drawing on studies from a variety of disciplines. Even academics who argue vociferously against Diamond's conclusions cannot help but marvel at the scope of his research. Similarly, a teacher of science may not always agree with a student's conclusions, but the teacher can certainly assess the extent to which the student provided adequate, valid supporting arguments.

In many ways, persuasive writing forces students to weigh evidence, to reflect, and to critically assess implications. In other words, persuasive writing pushes students to consider science-in-action.

Is it better for a woman to give birth naturally or via a Caesarian section? What is the universe made of? How long can a human being live? What would be the best plan for supplying water to a large city in the middle of a desert? These are the type of questions that require significant thought and effort and require a persuasive response.

NARRATIVE WRITING (ALSO KNOWN AS "TO CONVEY EXPERIENCE")

A third kind of writing used to be called narrative or "storytelling" (National Assessment of Educational Progress, 1997), but is now known by the moniker, "to convey experience." While writing that conveys experience is not emphasized as much as persuasive or informative writing in standards documents, conveying experience has been a primary function of writing, at least since around 2500 BCE.

Recently, the NAEP broadened the scope of what had been called *narrative* to encompass imagined experiences, leaving open the possibility for assignments that are exploratory or experimental. Einstein's famous vision that lead to the theory of relativity, in which he rides at the speed of light alongside a light beam (Stinnis & Metz, 2004) would qualify as a kind of "thought experiment" that would convey *imagined* experience. When the term *narrative* is used in this book, it will be the broadened sense of the word, including *conveying experience, real and imagined*.

Despite their distinctive traits, the three types of writing required by Common Core—persuasive, informative, and narrative—are not mutually exclusive.

For example, in the book *Complications* (2008), Dr. Atwul Gawande describes an encounter with a 400-pound compulsive eater with multiple health, psychological, and personal problems. In the course of telling the story, Gawande discusses the biological basis of hunger, the digestive system, the stress that obesity places on the body, and intricate details of gastric bypass surgery. Certainly, Gawande's narrative about "The man who couldn't stop eating" is informative, but it also persuades. After reading the story, most readers will be convinced that obesity is unhealthy, socially debilitating, and potentially deadly.

Expressive Writing

Of course, many different kinds of writing exist beyond the "big three" pantheon of persuasive, informative, and narrative writing. The most obvious exclusion from the pantheon is expressive writing, the kind of writing that frequently fills diaries and shows up on social media sites, such as Facebook.

7

Expressive writing, or "writing what you think" may not seem substantial at first blush, but writing expressively is often a necessary first step to more complex assignments. Here is how expressive writing might work in a class on friction and the laws of motion.

Figure 4. How a science teacher might use expressive writing.

After discussing the concept of friction and the laws of motion in class, a teacher decides to conduct a brief experiment. So, she brings to class a golf ball, a steel ball bearing, and a glass bowl. First, she spins the golf ball in the glass bowl and measures the time it takes for the golf ball to stop spinning. She announces the time and writes it on the board.

She asks students, "Take three minutes and explain what is happening in this glass bowl in terms of the golf ball, friction, and the laws of motion."

After three minutes, she asks a few students to read what they have written aloud. At this point, most students in class may be tentative, so the teacher highlights student comments that are accurate and corrects student comments that are not, revisiting Newton's laws of motion when appropriate.

Then, she holds up the steel ball bearing and asks, "What is going to happen when I spin the steel ball bearing in the bowl? Will it spin for a longer or shorter time? Make a prediction of how long it sill spin and explain why in terms of friction and the laws of motion. Take 3 minutes to write a prediction and a rationale."

Before spinning the steel ball in the glass bowl, the teacher asks several students to read aloud their predictions and rationales. Then, she spins the steel ball bearing in the glass bowl, announces the elapsed time, writes it on the board next to the golf ball's time, congratulates students with the most accurate predictions, and makes some final points. These two expressive, quick-writes would require students to apply their knowledge to a new situation, obliging them to conduct a mini-thought experiment of sorts. Such assignments can serve as prelude to a subsequent, more formal experiment and report.

The teacher says, "Please turn in your quickwrite. I will give them a 'quickcheck' to see how well you are understanding friction and the laws of motion." After class, the teacher scans student papers and gives a "check" in the gradebook to denote completion of the task. Alternatively, the teacher could have asked students to keep their papers in notebooks, which the teacher would pick up occasionally (unannounced) to monitor student participation and comprehension.

Before asking students to complete a formal writing task, such as a persuasive essay or an informative research paper, it may be beneficial for them to first have accumulated a series of non-graded, expressive, quick-writes. Then, when the longer paper is assigned, students have a ready-made pile of writing upon which to draw. This manner of using more informal assignments to provide a foundation for subsequent, more formal writing avoids the "terror of the blank page" syndrome.

When students in class despair that, "I don't know what to write" in response to an assignment, it is usually because they have not yet decided what they think. Expressive writing helps students decide what they think and makes the jump to more complex writing less daunting.

Even the NAEP acknowledges the centrality of expressive writing.

Many writing situations encourage students to write as a means of self-expression and comprehension, as is the case with writing-to-learn activities when the student composes as a means of thinking through key ideas on a topic. The importance of written communication for personal purposes cannot be overstated: students given adequate practice in developing their own thoughts and feelings through such writing are better able to perform well in all forms of writing. (National Assessment of Educational Progress, 2010, pp. 3-4)

It is unreasonable to expect students to instantly write as if they were experts about a new concept within the time limitations of a class or two. Expressive writing provides the scaffolding necessary for students to move from vague ideas to knowledge and application.

CREATIVE WRITING AND MIXED MEDIA

Students need exposure to different kinds of writing. A steady diet of informative writing and nothing but informative writing might not be optimal for a student's cognitive development. Assigning a variety of writing tasks—expressive, narrative, persuasive, informative—is a good way to help insure students learn how to write for different purposes. However, beyond these essential forms of writing, a teacher may consider other, creative possibilities that do not fall neatly into any single category. Creative writing does not have to involve writing short stories; it can be any kind of composition that does not fit neatly into a particular category.

Mixed media writing, which combines various kinds of writing with electronic media, gets easier with each new wave of technological advance. Armed with a simple cell phone, it is possible to combine drawings with narrative text, photographs with informational text, film with persuasive text, audio with expressive text, or myriad other combinations.

In many ways, mixed media writing is the future. Consider the following statistics about the popular video site, Youtube (YouTube, 2013).

- More than 1 billion unique users visit YouTube each month
- Over 6 billion hours of video are watched each month on YouTube, or about an hour of video viewing for every person on earth
- 100 hours of video are uploaded to YouTube every minute
- 70% of YouTube traffic comes from outside the US
- YouTube exists in 56 countries and across 61 languages
- YouTube reaches more US adults ages 18-34 than any cable network

One of the great strengths of visual media is that they are able to imbue a message with clarity and power. High school science teacher Greg Craven posted a short,

9

homemade video entitled "The most terrifying video you'll ever see" on Youtube in 2007. Within six months, the video received more than four million viewings (Knickerbocker, 2007) and Craven was offered a book contract from Penguin, which eventually resulted in *What's the worst that could happen?* (Craven, 2009).

Writing assignments could take a variety of forms, including:

- quickwrite
- journal entry
- blog
- summary
- lab report
- story
- informative essay
- persuasive essay
- research paper
- script
- website
- film
- speech
- presentation
- mixed media experience
- book
- magazine
- brochure
- poster
- newsletter
- other

To expand a student's audience for writing beyond the teacher-as-evaluator is a potent idea that can genuinely foster student engagement. For a group research project, a teacher might ask each group of students to film their oral presentations and post them on Youtube, Vimeo, or another video website so that students in other classes, parents, and friends could see them. In this book, all graded (level 3) writing assignments involve mixed-media.

SPECIFY THE AUDIENCE

Think about how differently you would communicate a description of a recent car accident to different audiences—a classroom of second graders at a local elementary school, a buddy at a nightclub, and the insurance adjuster at his office. If you want students to create a brilliant, in-depth piece of writing, they are going to need to know for whom they are writing. In most science classrooms, 100% of assignments are created for an audience of one—the teacher—who typically evaluates a paper for correctness and then assigns a grade. However, a teacher need not serve as the sole-evaluator-in-residence for every writing assignment.

Sometimes, students could write to the teacher-as-editor to receive friendly advice on what to improve before re-submitting a paper for a grade. Or, students could write for their peers in class, parents, a general audience on the web, students in a sixth grade class in Mexico City, or the board of directors at NASA (National Aeronautics and Space Administration).

Some creative science teachers routinely require students to read papers to non-science-oriented adults, such as an English teacher, an uncle, or the custodian. Implementing this innovation is easy and straightforward. Students simply give a one-page form to a listener to complete. The LOC (listener-out-of-class) form asks the listener to rate the quality of the student's oral delivery, clarity of expression, and ability to answer questions. See an example of the form in Figure 5.

Figure 5. Listener Out-of-Class (LOC).

Student name_____ Date_____

Your name_____
Occupation_____

Students in _____'s science class must read their papers aloud to a variety of audiences. Congratulations! You have been chosen as an audience! Thanks for helping.

Your honest assessment of this written response will help establish the student's understanding of concepts and ideas covered in class. The entire assessment should take less than 5 minutes.

Write answers below. When you are done, please give the form back to the student, who will return the form to the teacher. Additional comments and questions are welcome.

1. Summarize the main idea of the passage that the student read aloud. You may ask the student to re-read the passage or to elaborate on any part of it.

2. Pose a question to the student related to this piece of writing. Please write the question below.

3. Summarize the student's response to the question.

4. Additional comments?

THANK YOU.

Teacher's name
School
Email address
Telephone number

The entire interchange between student and adult listener should take five minutes or less. The listener writes down student responses, hands the form back to the student, who turns it in to the teacher. Providing an "outside audience" gives students the chance to translate scientific concepts into everyday language, which, in turn, helps enhance understanding. Additional advantages of using an audience other than teacher-as-evaluator include:

1. The LOC one-pager provides a checkpoint for student mastery of a concept
2. The LOC one-pager provides an audience other than teacher-as-evaluator
3. The LOC one-pager is completed by listening adults, thereby reducing the paper load of the teacher.

Audience influences word choice, sentence structure, organization, and most aspects of writing. Before beginning to write, it would be useful to know for whom the writing is intended. Some possible audiences include:

> teacher as evaluator (graded)
> teacher as writing coach (non-graded)
> other teachers
> family members
> social workers
> chamber of commerce
> science fair judges
> peers
> a hostile audience
> online general audience
> experts
> novices
> younger audiences (for example, third graders at a nearby school)
> older audiences (for example, individuals living in a retirement home)
> non-native speakers
> other

A final consideration for audience is the decision for the student concerning whether or not to seek publication. Print and online magazines eagerly accept submissions and having a student's work appear in a high-visibility publication can be a boon to the student, parents, teacher, and school.

SELECT THE MEDIUM

The traditional writing assignment in science has been text and nothing but text. However, other possibilities abound—film, websites, presentations, podcasts, mixed media, even theatrical performance (see Tom Stoppard's *Arcadia* for an example of a recent theatrical production in which science plays a prominent role). At the least, a teacher should consider requiring students to supplement textual reports with images and/or sound.

DETERMINE THE LENGTH OF TIME STUDENTS GET TO WRITE

Quickwrites are usually done spontaneously and completed in a matter of minutes. The NAEP writing assessment, as with most writing assessments, usually give students about 30 minutes to complete an essay. Longer research papers may take anywhere from a few days to several weeks to complete. The range of times designated for assignments over the course of a term might include writing completed in:

3 minutes
30 minutes
One day (due at the end of the period)
Several days
Two weeks
A semester

As with purpose and audience, the best approach may be to expose students to a variety of timed writing experiences. Some writing may be done quickly and handed in immediately with no chance for revision. Other writing may entail significant amounts of research, require multiple drafts, and necessitate revision outside of class.

OTHER FACTORS

The life of a teacher is greatly simplified if he/she decides that the default for writing assignments is that they will be graded on "completion." Basically, this translates into giving students credit for thinking through the written word. If students can get used to articulating what they think, then it becomes easier for a teacher to discern when a student gets lost or misconstrues a concept. Also, it allows for greater accuracy when attempting to scaffold student learning.

This kind of formative assessment also prevents every writing assignment from turning into a time-consuming, tension-inducing ordeal. If the default for a writing assignment is non-graded, then a teacher can scan what has been written and offer a quick response. If concern grows that students are not taking the non-graded writing assignment seriously enough, then selecting a random written response for-a-grade is always an option.

Another factor, the collaborative nature of learning, has become a hot topic in education circles (Day & Bryce, 2013; Topping, Thurston, Tolmie, Christie, Murray, & Karagiannidou, 2011). While students can definitely benefit from participating as part of a larger group, particularly when engaging in research, relying solely upon a group grade for writing is not best practice—for several reasons. First, in life, as in the classroom, there are always students who will strive for the "highest possible grade" for the "lowest possible effort." To combat this tendency, a teacher must keep students culpable for their individual performance, as well as their contribution as part of a larger team. Thus, when working with groups, taking both an individual grade and a group grade is a good idea.

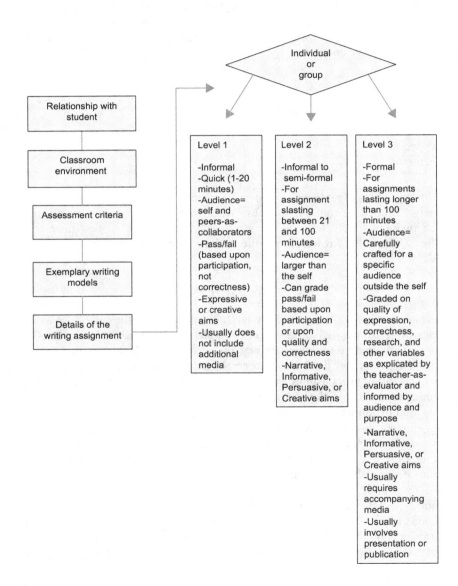

FLOWCHART FOR WRITING

The foundation for writing in science is the teacher's relationship with the student (Stormer, 2013). If the student trusts and respects the teacher, then much can be accomplished. If the student does not trust or respect the teacher, however, the student may be reluctant to write or to put forth much effort. Certainly, the profusion of studies supporting the influence of non-cognitive factors on learning must be given serious consideration (Farrington, Roderick, Allensworth, Nagaoka, Keyes, Johnson, & Beechum, 2012).

Related to the teacher's relationship to the student is the environment of the classroom. The physical environment can act as continuous teacher's aide, stimulating interest in science and helping students learn. Conversely, with barren walls and a dearth of gadgets, charts, recent books, magazines, and pictures, the physical classroom can act as an inhibitor. A science teacher with a sufficiently large room may designate specific spaces for "new books," reading silently, writing, discussion, tools, model student papers, or poster-building (as well as a snack bar).

For writing assignments lasting more than a few minutes, the criteria upon which the paper will be assessed should be clear. Indeed, the act of specifying what a piece of writing should contain is, in itself, a highly effective way of improving the quality of student papers (Hillocks, 1986, 1999). The idea is to demystify good writing by giving students an explicit, step-by-step guide.

Perhaps one of the most frustrating aspects of contemporary schooling for students is the dearth of models of what is considered stellar work. When trying to build anything from scratch, from a bicycle to a research brief, it helps to have a model handy to guide the effort. A word of caution: a student's very first exposure to a model has the power to forever imprint it as a prototype, so the model needs to be good. The best kind of model is a student-penned A+ paper, but examples from professional writers or from teachers will work, too. It is beneficial for students to know what "satisfactory" looks like.

One of the first decisions about making a writing assignment is determining if students will work individually or as part of a larger group. Writing of both types will be expected of students beyond high school.

A second decision is to decide on the scope of the assignment, or the level of writing.

LEVELS OF WRITING

A **level one** writing assignment may involve a simple, 3-minute, expressive, "quickwrite." Possible goals might be to help frame a topic, to assess initial understanding, to encourage speculation, or to have students attempt to discern what they think. For example, if studying taxonomy, the teacher might show a picture of a Green Sea Slug and ask if it should be classified as a plant or an animal (chapter 7). A teacher may discuss with students the characteristics of plants and animals, then assign a quickwrite, asking students to explore their thoughts on the matter.

Although it is almost always beneficial to have students read aloud their quickwrites, the usual audience for such an assignment is the self. The purpose of a quickwrite may be to give students the opportunity to capture their thoughts at a particular moment in time and put them into words. Without the time to reflect, scientific concepts can quickly turn into confused notions and fuzzy recollections.

The teacher rarely grades a level one writing assignment. Rather, it is a tool to check comprehension or to help direct thinking in particular ways. In fact, a teacher may assign several quickwrites for various purposes within a single class period.

Unlike the level one assignment, the **level three** writing assignment requires significant thought, time, effort, and attention to the metrics of evaluation. The purpose of most level three writing is to inform or persuade a specific audience through both substance and style. Presentation or publication is often integrated into the evaluation. Level three writing is intense and time-consuming, thus should be assigned sparingly.

A **level two** writing assignment is somewhere between a quickwrite and a lengthy research paper. A teacher may want students to expound upon a previous quickwrite, go a little deeper, or start to build materials for a longer research paper. The Figure 7 below summarizes some of the characteristics of each kind of writing.

Figure 7. Levels of writing

Level	1	2	3
Formality	Informal	Informal to semi-formal	Formal
Individual/group	Individual	Individual or group	Individual or group
Time to complete the assignment	Less than 20 minutes	21 to 100 minutes	More than 100 minutes
Assessment	Participation only	Either participation or graded	Graded
Research	No	Possibly some	Yes
Presentation	Informal read aloud	Sometimes	Yes
Frequency of assignment	Daily	Whenever it can be fit into the schedule	From two weeks to a semester
Purpose	Usually Expressive	Narrative (conveying experience), Persuasive, Informative, or Creative	Narrative, Persuasive, Informative, or Creative
Audience	Self	Specific or general audience outside the self	Very specific
Medium	Usually text, sometimes text and images	Open or directed	Usually text plus charts, tables, images, and artifacts

The following twelve tips in Figure 8 summarize some major points about assigning writing.

Figure 8. Twelve tips for integrating writing into science

1. Create easy and attractive entry points. Add complexity over time.
2. Vary the stimulus. Have students write for informative, persuasive, expressive, narrative (conveying experience), and creative purposes for variable amounts of time (short, long, in-class, out-of-class, group, individual) for different audiences.
3. Use level one quickwrites and level two, non-graded writing as building blocks to longer, level three writing assignments.
4. Find current articles/books that you find interesting and bring them to class. Read aloud the text (or parts of it) in class. Explain why you find the topic interesting. Point out a sentence or two that you find eloquent.
5. Designate places in your classroom to display recent articles/books as well as model papers.
6. For level 2 and level 3 papers longer than a page, specify the audience. Encourage audiences other than the teacher-as-evaluator.
7. As much as possible, require students to integrate multisensory components, such as images, sound, charts, and video into their oral presentations. Encourage students to consider the aesthetics of their final, level 3 papers.
8. Plan for blocks of time when students focus entirely on writing.
9. Vary the medium (not just reports, but also videos, photos, presentations, brochures, and stories).
10. Assign some writing that must be completed as a group. Allow time for students to talk about their writing project with other members of their group. Set deadlines and specify individual responsibilities. Assess both individual and group performance.
11. Have students read aloud and do presentations as a matter-of-course.
12. Don't grade everything. Spot check longer papers.

ASSESSING WRITING WHILE
MAINTAINING SANITY

Most science teachers may not find the prospect of adding piles of quickwrites and research papers onto an already heavy load of planning, lab work, teaching, and "extra-curricular responsibilities as needed" particularly enticing. For a science teacher with five classes of thirty students each, assigning a research project would mean grading 150 papers. Taking only ten minutes per paper would mean the expenditure of 1500 minutes, or a cool 25 hours of work.

However, there are ways to reduce the time spent evaluating papers, some of which were mentioned in the previous chapter.

1. Selectively choose assignments that will be graded; allowing other assignments to be part of the "science notebook"
2. Use a check system whereby the teacher quickly marks whether or not a specific part of a longer paper has been completed
3. Distribute the audience (peers, parents, other adults, experts, or review boards)
4. Assess oral presentations of written documents
5. Require students to write, edit, and seek approval for papers during class time.

A friend who teaches biology at a local high school is a strong advocate for requiring students to write, edit, and discuss papers during class time (number 5 above). He insists that science is not a halfway game; there are few halfway right answers, so, he will only allow students to move ahead to the next section of a paper after the previous section has been approved—and the baseline for approval is the grade of A. So, students who do not satisfactorily complete a section of the paper receive a zero. The only possible grades on any writing assignment are zero or A. While such a grading scheme may seem draconian, students have responded well to the challenge. Failures in his class are rare.

Part of his secret is that he encourages students to get help from peers and other adults as well as through his frequent mini-conferences in class. Not only do the students learn to write well, he claims that he never takes a paper home to grade.

VALID AND RELIABLE ASSESSMENT

One of the truths about writing in science is that it substantially limits the amount of insincere blather (also known as bullshit) that can emanate from the mind of a student when he/she has absolutely no idea about a correct response. A student who does not have a basic understanding of scientific theories will have immense difficulty in applying them. In responding to an authentic scientific problem through an essay, there is no way to "luck out" on a guess at the correct answer; there is no place to hide. In general, essays that require students to invoke pertinent scientific principles and theories and to explore potential applications are more genuine assessments of student knowledge than objective tests of short queries paired with possible answers already furnished.

Another advantage of writing essays is that the teacher can get a sense of where student comprehension is strong and where understanding begins to break down. After all, writing is a form of concretized thought. Thus, when a student's grasp of a concept begins to get off-track, it is only through those moments when thought is made visible that a teacher is able to identify the problem and provide help. Writing provides the opportunity for the kind of intervention that can prevent conceptual misunderstandings that can haunt a student for his entire academic career. Indeed, Heddy & Sinatra (2013) and Francek (2013) have found that one of the most difficult areas of teaching is trying to get students to un-learn a misconception.

MYSTERY ASSESSMENTS

Imagine taking a team of students to a science fair, then having the judges of the competition change the criteria on which projects were to be judged after your team arrives. Then, ten minutes later, the judges decide to alter their scoring rubric again, though they refuse to reveal how the criteria have changed or even what new criteria might be used. The response of most teachers would be total frustration and a pledge to never again enter any students into this particular science fair competition.

Unfortunately, many science teachers utilize a similar kind of "mystery evaluation system" as a matter of course in their classes. Too often, students do not understand the criteria upon which they are to be graded before they undertake a project. Unfortunately, students do not have the option of choosing another science fair. Instead, they must accept whatever system the teacher decides to adopt, even if it may be invalid, unreliable, and amorphous.

The moral is that the criteria upon which a particular assignment will be assessed should be given to students when making the assignment—not revealed to them afterwards. What is important? What is superfluous? What should the student be able to do upon completion of the assignment? What is the purpose? Framing an assignment by revealing the criteria by which it will be graded helps students know where to focus their energies.

Indeed, one of the most effective approaches to improve the quality of writing is to identify the characteristics of good writing and insert them into the evaluation. In this manner, students who write to get a high grade actualize the desired effective strategies to do so. In the parlance of some composition studies (Hillocks, 1986, 2011), such an approach to writing is sometimes called *scalar* because the grading scale helps direct student effort.

Once a student knows what is expected, the probability that their eventual academic efforts will approximate the desired result is infinitely greater than when writing under a mysterious grading rubric.

THE CRITERIA FOR WRITING ASSESSMENTS

The NAEP (National Assessment of Educational Progress), who has been evaluating the writing of American students since 1969 (Stedman, 2009), suggests basic criteria for making writing assignments. A teacher should specify TAP—Topic, Audience, and Purpose—for most formal writing assignments. The topic should address" real-world, age-appropriate, and grade-appropriate issues" (National Assessment Governing Board, 2010, p. 6) and be open enough to allow for some student choice and the exercise of creativity.

The audience should be specified for every assignment as well and should also be age-appropriate and familiar enough to students so that they can organize their papers accordingly. For example, having students prepare papers for a professional group of phlebotomists, members of medical laboratory teams who collect and transport laboratory specimens, may not be appropriate because students would be uncertain of the plebotanist's daily work and possible frames of reference. However, designating a "general audience" that includes peers, parents, and other adults interested in health issues would be fair and appropriate.

The NAEP uses a set of basic criteria to score essays, with elaborations that vary with TAP (topic, audience, purpose).

Figure 9. NAEP Basic Criteria (National Assessment Governing Board, 2010)

I. Idea development (in relation to TAP)
   Depth and complexity
   Details
   Examples
   Effectiveness

II. Organization (in relation to TAP)
   Structure
   Coherence
   Focus
   Transitions

III. Mastery of the language (in relation to TAP)
   Sentence structure and variety
   Word choice
   Voice and tone
   Grammar, mechanics, usage

Six-point grading scale

The typical NAEP evaluation tool ranks student writing on a scale from 0 to 6, with 0 meaning that the student turned in a blank page and a 6 representing the highest possible score. The easiest way to translate NAEP scores for the traditional grading scale is as follows:

   6=A
   5=B
   4=C
   3=D+
   2=D-
   1=F

The lowest possible passing score is a 4, sufficient. Scores of 3, 2, or 1 are failing in that the writing does not meet a minimum standard. Sometimes, the NAEP presents results using the following scale:

   Advanced
   Proficient
   Basic
   Below basic

The logical letter grade correlation to each category is:

Advanced=A
Proficient=B
Basic=C
Below basic=D or F

The six-point scale is preferable to a four-point scale because it provides more information for students who need it the most—those scoring 1, 2, and 3. A student who scores a 3 on an assignment may be centimeters from a passing score, whereas a student who scores a 1 could be light years away from a passing score. A four-point scale places the student who scores a 3 in the same category as the student who scores a 1—"below basic." Students who fail to meet the minimum standard need to know precisely what they need to do to bring the quality of their writing up to a passing score.

HOW TO SCORE WRITING

If you were going to be trained to score writing for NAEP, you would be placed into a group and given the criteria for scoring a specific kind of writing. Following a discussion of the criteria, you would receive sample papers at each level, from A-F (or 6 to zero). These are called *benchmark* papers and are used to help make decisions for subsequent papers.

Then, you would receive a stack of papers to score. After you read a paper, you would place it in a pile of papers you think deserve a similar score. After you have placed all papers in the appropriate piles, A, B, C, D+, D-, and F, you would check to see how well your assessments align with other members in the group. If all of your assessments align well, then you would be allowed to continue to score papers for the NAEP. If one of your scores differed from the group by 1 point, that is, if you scored a paper an A-level, but everyone else scored it at the B-level, you would discuss the differences with the group leader and would be placed "on probation." If your scores eventually aligned with the group, then you would remain an NAEP scorer. If your scores continued to vary by a point, you would be let go.

If your score differed from the group by two levels, that is, if you scored a paper as an A-level, but everyone else scored it at the C-level, you would be dismissed.

The holistic method of scoring works well for most teachers as they have no problem distinguishing an A from a C or an F. The strength of the holistic approach is that it insures consistency, but also allows the teacher to focus on primary traits, or specific characteristics. When writing is assigned, strongly consider whether or not it needs to be graded. Most writing can be quickly scanned and given a ✓ (check mark) based upon completion. When an assignment needs to be graded, a holistic, primary-trait scoring format that utilizes a 6-point scale is recommended.

Three formal, level 3 rating scales for persuasive, narrative, and informational writing follow.

23

Figure 10. Rating scale for persuasive writing (NAEP, 2000), level 3

A=Excellent Takes a clear position and supports it consistently with well-chosen reasons and/or examples; may use persuasive strategy to convey an argument. Is focused and well organized, with effective use of transitions. Consistently exhibits variety in sentence structure and precision in word choice. Errors in grammar, spelling, and punctuation are few and do not interfere with understanding.
B=Skillful Takes a clear position and supports it with pertinent reasons and/or examples through much of the response. Is well organized, but may lack some transitions. Exhibits some variety in sentence structure and uses good word choice; occasionally, words may be used inaccurately. Errors in grammar, spelling, and punctuation do not interfere with understanding.
C=Sufficient Takes a clear position and supports it with some pertinent reasons and/or examples; there is some development. Is generally organized, but has few or no transitions among parts. Sentence structure may be simple and unvaried; word choice is mostly accurate. Errors in grammar, spelling, and punctuation do not interfere with understanding.
D+=Uneven (may be characterized by one or more of the following:) Takes a position and provides uneven support; may lack development in parts or be repetitive OR response is no more than a well-written beginning. Is organized in parts of the response; other parts are disjointed and/or lack transitions. Exhibits uneven control over sentence boundaries and sentence structure; may exhibit some inaccurate word choices. Errors in grammar, spelling, and punctuation sometimes interfere with understanding.
D-=Insufficient (may be characterized by one or more of the following:) Takes a position but is very undeveloped. Is disorganized or unfocused in much of the response OR clear but very brief. Minimal control over sentence boundaries and sentence structure; word choice may often be inaccurate. Errors in grammar, spelling, and punctuation interfere with understanding in much of the response.
F=Unsatisfactory (may be characterized by one or more of the following:) Attempts to take a position (addresses topic) but position is very unclear OR takes a position, but provides minimal or no support; may only paraphrase the prompt. Exhibits little or no apparent organization. Minimal or no control over sentence boundaries and sentence structure; word choice may be inaccurate in much or all of the response. Errors in grammar, spelling, and punctuation severely impede understanding across the response.

Figure 11. Rating scale for narrative writing (NAEP, 1999), level 3

A=Excellent
Tells a clear story that is consistently well-developed and detailed; details enhance story being told.   Well organized; integrates narrative events into a smooth telling; effective transitions move the story forward.   Consistently exhibits variety in sentence structure and precision in word choice.   Errors in grammar, spelling, and punctuation are few and do not interfere with understanding.
B=Skillful
Tells a clear story that is well-developed and supported with pertinent details in much of the response.   Well organized with story elements connected across most of the response; may have occasional lapses in transitions.   Exhibits some variety in sentence structure and uses good word choice; occasionally, words may be used inaccurately.   Errors in grammar, spelling, and punctuation do not interfere with understanding.
C=Sufficient
Tells a clear story that is developed with some pertinent details.   Generally organized, but transitions between parts of the story may be lacking.   Sentence structure may be simple and unvaried; word choice is mostly accurate.   Errors in grammar, spelling, and punctuation do not interfere with understanding.
D+=Uneven (may be characterized by one or more of the following:)
Tells a story that may be clear and developed in parts; other parts are unfocused, repetitive, or minimally developed, OR is no more than a well-written beginning.   Organized in parts of the response; other parts are disjointed or lack transitions.   Exhibits uneven control over sentence boundaries and sentence structure; may exhibit some inaccurate word choices.   Errors in grammar, spelling, and punctuation sometimes interfere with understanding.
D-=Insufficient (may be characterized by one or more of the following:)
Attempts to tell a story, but is very undeveloped, listlike, or fragmentary.   Disorganized or unfocused in much of the response, OR the response is too brief to detect organization.   Minimal control over sentence boundaries and sentence structure; word choice may often be inaccurate.   Errors in grammar, spelling, and punctuation interfere with understanding in much of the response.
F=Unsatisfactory (may be characterized by one or more of the following:)
Responds to prompt but provides little or no coherent content, OR merely paraphrases the prompt.   Little or no apparent organization.   Minimal or no control over sentence boundaries and sentence structure; word choice may be inaccurate in much or all of the response.   Errors in grammar, spelling, and punctuation severely impede understanding across the response.

Figure 12. Rating scale for informative writing (NAEP, 1999), level 3

A=Excellent
Information is presented effectively and consistently supported with well-chosen details. Focused and well organized, with a sustained controlling idea and effective use of transitions. Consistently exhibits variety in sentence structure and precision in word choice; word choice enhances understanding. Errors in grammar, spelling, and punctuation are few and do not interfere with understanding.
B=Skillful
Information is presented clearly and supported with pertinent details in much of the response. Well organized, but may lack some transitions. Exhibits some variety in sentence structure and uses good word choice. Errors in grammar, spelling, and punctuation do not interfere with understanding.
C=Sufficient
Information is presented clearly and supported with some pertinent details. Generally organized, but has few or no transitions between parts. Sentence structure may be simple and unvaried; word choice is mostly accurate. Errors in grammar, spelling, and punctuation do not interfere with understanding.
D+=Uneven (may be characterized by one or more of the following:)
Information is presented clearly in parts; other parts are undeveloped or repetitive, OR is no more than a well-written beginning. Organized in parts of the response; other parts are disjointed or lack transitions. Exhibits uneven control over sentence boundaries and sentence structure; may exhibit some inaccurate word choices. Errors in grammar, spelling, and punctuation sometimes interfere with understanding.
D-=Insufficient (may be characterized by one or more of the following:)
Provides information that is very undeveloped or listlike. Disorganized or unfocused in much of the response, OR is too brief to detect organization. Minimal control over sentence boundaries and sentence structure; word choice may often be inaccurate. Errors in grammar, spelling, and punctuation interfere with understanding in much of the response.
F=Unsatisfactory (may be characterized by one or more of the following:)
Responds to prompt but may be incoherent, OR provides very minimal information, OR merely paraphrases the prompt. Little or no apparent organization. Minimal or no control over sentence boundaries and sentence structure; word choice may be inaccurate in much or all of the response. Errors in grammar, spelling, and punctuation severely impede understanding across the response.

GOING VIRAL

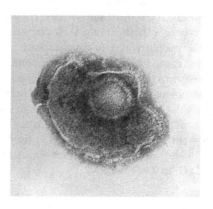

INTRODUCTION

Microbiomes comprise about half of earth's biomass. Without microbiomes, many organisms would cease to exist.

The microbiome can be defined as a collection of bacteria, bacteriophage, fungi, protozoa and/or viruses. The Human Microbiome Project seeks to discover a "core" microbiome and to analyze variation and function. The HMP, which has obvious connections to the HGP (Human Genome Project) states that:

> Within the human body, it is estimated that there are 10x as many microbial cells as human cells. Our microbial partners carry out a number of metabolic reactions that are not encoded in the human genome and are necessary for human health. Therefore when we talk about the "human genome" we should think of it as an amalgam of human genes and those of our microbes.
> (National Institutes of Health Human Microbiome Project, 2013)

Data about the human microbiome are fascinating. For example, the Human Microbiome Project found that a teaspoon of seawater may contain as many as 1,000,000 viruses (Schors, 2013, p. 3). Humans are exposed to millions of viruses each day and relatively few actually make us sick. Kolata (2012) writes:

> In a new five-year federal endeavor, the Human Microbiome Project, which has been compared to the Human Genome Project, 200 scientists at 80 institutions sequenced the genetic material of bacteria taken from nearly 250 healthy people. They discovered more strains than they had ever imagined—as many

as a thousand bacterial strains on each person. And each person's collection of microbes, the microbiome, was different from the next person's.

The website Medpage Today (www.medpage.com), a free, "trusted news service for physicians that provides a clinical perspective on the breaking medical news," routinely features news about the devastating effects of various viruses. Recently, bulletins have been issued on West Nile Virus, Coranavirus (a newly discovered virus possibly originating in the Middle East), HIV, Bird Flu, herpes, chickenpox, and Hepatitis C. However, virologists have been experimenting with engineering viruses for healthy ends as well. For example, people with eye diseases such as macular degeneration and retinitis pigmentosa that cause vision impairment or blindness have had their sight restored using an engineered virus (Beltran, et al., 2012; Cepko & Vandenberghe, 2013).

Certainly, the immense power of the microbiome has been cultivated by writers, such as Stephen King, who describes a rampant flu virus in *The Stand*; Robin Cook, who charts the progress of the deadly Ebola Hemorrhagic Fever in *Contagion*; Michael Crichton, who writes of a viral threat that originated in outer space in *Andromeda Strain*; and Richard Preston, who writes about an incredible, real Ebola outbreak in Washington D.C. in *The Hot Zone*.

RESEARCH ON USING WRITING TO TEACH MICROBIOLOGY

"By blending storytelling with topics in biology, a fun activity can be created for students to strengthen their scientific knowledge" (Dolberry, 2010, p. 175).

"Despite substantial evidence that writing can be an effective tool in student learning and engagement…and that WTL [writing to learn] strategies can enhance knowledge acquisition and cognitive skill development in science disciplines, WTL practices are still not widely implemented" (Reynolds, Thaiss, Katkin, & Thompson, 2012, p. 17).

"By blending storytelling with topics in biology, a fun activity can be created for students to strengthen their scientific knowledge" (Blankinship, 2011, p. 175).

As a result of a writing-intensive, project approach to the study of microbes, "ninety-one percent of students demonstrated increased knowledge of microbial concepts and methods" (Burleson & Martinez-Vaz, 2011, p. 2).

RESEARCH ON "LEARNING BY DESIGN" IN MICROBIOLOGY

Learning by design "engages students in the type of critical thinking and problem-solving increasingly emphasized in science education." (Kuniyuki & Sharp, 2011, p. 141)

"We engage our students in the concepts of testability, falsifiability, and repeatability by asking them to try to disprove discoveries of the past" (Cherif, Siuda, & Mozahedzadeh, 2013, p. 14).

"In 2003, they [Venter and Smith] developed a new method to assemble fragments of DNA and built their first virus; when that worked, they scaled up to bacteria, ultimately writing their names and quotes in its code" (Hylton, 2012).

COMMENTS ON MICROBIOLOGY

"Today, biomedical science sits on the cusp of another revolution: the use of human and microbial cells as therapeutic entities." (Fischbach, Bluestone, & Lim, 2013, p. 1)

"The HMP was designed in part to address a key question about our microbial selves: do all humans have an identifiable 'core' microbiome of shared components comparable to our shared genome?" (Gevers, Knight, Petrosinio, Huang, McGuire, Birren, Nelson, White, Methé, & Huttenhower, 2012, p. 3)

"The HMP will not only identify new ways to determine health and predisposition to diseases but also define the parameters needed to design, implement and monitor strategies for intentionally manipulating the human microbiota, to optimize its performance in the context of an individual's physiology" (Turnbaugh, Ley, Hamady, Fraser-Liggett, Knight, & Gordon, 2007, p. 804)

"The study of indigenous populations can provide insights into human behaviors that define human microbiome variation, such as non-industrialized subsistence and the functional potential of microbiomes before the potentially damaging effects of antibiotics. Human microbiomes from countries harboring traditional communities can be more diverse than those from countries strictly harboring cosmopolitan communities" (Lewis, Obregon-Tito, Tito, Foster, & Spicer, 2012, p. 2).

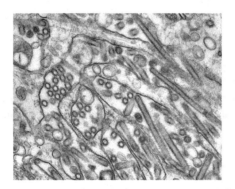

THE LESSON

Understanding the properties of a virus through study, analysis, research, and prediction.

29

ACTIVITY

Students learn the basic ways that a virus spreads and how it can be contained through analyzing the features of real-life viruses. Students create their own anti-virus, based upon their knowledge of how viruses invade human cells, and write an action plan for dealing with a potential pandemic outbreak of H5N1 (bird flu).

ANCHOR POINT

Students will get an idea of viruses, their functions, and how they affect us through firsthand experience or through media reports about the flu (influenza), HIV, herpes, Ebola, or other viral-related health issues. The instructor uses images (3-dimensional, if possible) to help students visualize viruses and how they interact with cells. These visualization strategies provide the anchor point.

CHALLENGE

It is difficult to study something that cannot be seen without the aid of a powerful electron microscope. Most viruses are just 1% of the size of bacteria. Placing viruses side-by-side (probably not a good idea), it would take as many as two million viruses to reach an inch. Thus, the challenge is to "bring to life" the importance of a tiny biological agent that plays an integral role in living matter.

TIMELINE

Days 1-2=Learning about the structure and variety of viruses, learning how viruses spread, group work on combating H5N1 Day 3=Presentations of action plans.

OBJECTIVE

Students will learn about viruses.

SUMMARY

The lesson involves direct instruction (learning about several different viruses), modeling (using what has been learned about viruses), application (relating knowledge to a new situation), and prediction (forecasting the effects of changes in viruses).

MATERIALS

Essentials include images of viruses, non-fiction books, fiction, drawing paper and crayons or felt-tip markers. The website http://ictvonline.org/index.asp provides access to a taxonomy of viruses and is frequently updated.

FIVE USEFUL WEBSITES

Microbiology overview that eventually gets to viruses:
http://www.youtube.com/watch?v=ThU9Ckp1mB8

Khan's Academy on viruses:
http://www.youtube.com/watch?v=0h5Jd7sgQWY&list=EC7A9646BC5110CF64
&index=19

Craig Savage, high school AP Biology teacher, intro to Viruses:
http://www.youtube.com/watch?v=PEWjyx2TkM8

Virtual "Immunology Lab" goes through the process of testing samples in disease diagnosis: http://www.hhmi.org/biointeractive/vlabs/immunology/index.html

"Microbes in Action" provides advice for lab experiments
http://www.umsl.edu/~microbes/index.html

SET-UP

When Craig Venter (Hylton, 2012) set out to build a synthetic organism from fragments of DNA, he began with a virus, then expanded his efforts to bacteria. A teacher might approach microbiology in the same way, by beginning with viruses, then moving to other parts of the microbiome. This lesson focuses on viruses, paving the way for a follow-up lesson that would examine bacteria and other microbiomes. Having images of viruses on-hand are necessary to give students a genuine sense of how viruses exist and interact with the human body.

PROCEDURE

1. Ask if anyone in class has been ill with a virus lately. Try to identify the specific virus at work—the flu, a cold, or an indeterminate virus. Identify symptoms, treatments (including medication), and effectiveness of the treatment.
2. Show students a variety of images of viruses. Ask students to note similarities in the appearance of the various viruses. The "Virusworld" website sponsored by the University of Wisconsin (http://www.virology.wisc.edu/virusworld/viruslist.php) has an extensive collection of images and movies, including: DNA (enveloped) viruses such as Hepatitis B and Herpes Simplex 1A and RNA (enveloped) viruses, such as HIV and Yellow fever.
3. Emphasize to students that a virus is only a fraction of the size of bacteria. Show the comparison chart at http://publications.nigms.nih.gov/chemhealth/cool.htm.
4. Discuss how a virus works. National Public Radio has a short video (under four minutes) that explains how a virus attacks human cells: http://www.npr.org/blogs/

krulwich/2011/06/01/114075029/flu-attack-how-a-virus-invades-your-body. The NSTA website has a useful handout that includes a "flip book," which shows step-by-step how a virus attacks a healthy cell at www.nsta.org/pdfs/virus/Virus-Activity1.pdf.

5. 3-MINUTE EXPRESSIVE QUICKWRITE, LEVEL 1 Students write a summary of how a virus attacks human cells in their own words.

6. Show the labeled image of a virus at http://www.bbc.co.uk/science/0/21143412. At a minimum, students should be able to identify these parts and their functions: surface proteins, viral envelope, capsid, genetic material (DNA or RNA) . An unlabeled, three-dimensional depiction of a flu virus is available at the Center for Disease Control's website at: http://www.cdc.gov/flu/images.htm.

7. INFORMATIVE ESSAY, LEVEL 2 Have students choose a virus, hand-draw, and label it. Students write an explanation of their drawing and describe the functions of each part of a virus. Stanford professor Robert Siegel teaches a course each year in which he requires students to build a three-dimensional representation of a specific virus (Cantor Arts Center, 2013). The ambitious teacher may want to require 3-dimensional models.

8. In writing about "bird flu," or the H5N1 virus, the World Health Organization warns:
   H5N1 avian influenza is an infectious disease of birds that can be spread to people, but is difficult to transmit from person to person. Almost all people with H5N1 infection have had close contact with infected birds or H5N1-contaminated environments. When people do become infected, the mortality rate is about 60% (World Health Organization, 2013).

   In particular, discuss with students the meaning of the phrase, "the mortality rate is about 60%." A map of the areas where humans are most at risk of contracting H5N1 is available at: http://www.news.ucdavis.edu/special_reports/avian_flu/map_data.lasso. If any students illustrated and wrote about H5N1, point out those drawings (or 3-d models).

9. One of the reasons that H5N1 has not yet become a pandemic is that the virus currently is not transmitted person-to-person. However, virologists have discovered a way to manipulate the virus so that it *could* be transmitted via person-to-person and were set to publish their findings in the journal *Science and Nature*. The U.S. government intervened and requested that such potentially catastrophic information not be published for public consumption (MacIver, 2011). After a brief ban, findings on how the virus could be mutated to spread from person-to-person were finally published (Walsh, 2012).

10. INFORMATIVE WRITING, LEVEL 3 Place students into groups of two or three. Tell students that the World Health organization (WHO) wants to prevent a pandemic of the bird flu. To insure that a pandemic does not occur, students must develop an action plan to prevent the spread of the disease. This action plan should include the following five parts (see also figure 13: Assessment for proposal to the WHO to contain H5N1):

   a. Description of how H5N1 invades cells

   b. Drawing depicting H5N1 invading cells with clear indication of the part of the process they wish to attack with their new, anti-viral drug

   c. Description of how the most popular antiviral drug for H5N1, Tamiflu (also known as oseltamivir) works. Note: Students are not allowed to simply replicate the action of Tamiflu, but should take a different approach. Deciding where and how to intervene in the process will force students to make predictions based upon their knowledge of viruses and how they are spread.

   d. Drawing and accompanying narrative explicating exactly how their anti-viral drug will work against H5N1. Benefits and disadvantages of the selected design should be included.

   e. Informative essay, level 3, explaining the details of an "on the ground" campaign to alert individuals around the world of a potential threat of H5N1. What should people do to avoid contracting the disease? Where are the most likely "hot-spots" for the disease? How will they "get the word out?" Possible strategies might include publicity campaigns (TV, Internet, newspaper, billboards, social media), creating brochures, or delivering hand sanitizer or other disease prevention supplies to individuals or companies throughout the world. Students should keep in mind cost, potential effectiveness, and feasibility.

11. Students make presentations to the teacher who, as fictional Chief Executive Officer of the World Health Organization, will decide, based upon an assessment of presentations, who gets the multi-million dollar contract to battle H5N1 for the world.

COMMENT

Going Viral requires students to know and apply their knowledge of viruses in a very real-world situation. The lesson also provides an opportunity for grand thought experiments about ways to battle potential deadly viruses through pharmacology and the dissemination of information.

ENRICHMENT

A study of bacteria, bacteriophage, or new developments in synthetic biology would make an appropriate lesson for students who are keenly interested in microbiology. Some of the information is simply incredible. For example, did you know that the average adult carries two to five pounds of bacteria on the body? Half of a fecal stool (poop) is not digested food, but "microbial biomass" (Kolata, 2012). What such information may lack in aesthetic appeal is more than made up for in its potential to advance our knowledge of how the microbiome functions (Borody & Khoruts, 2012). Consider that "fecal transplants," in which the poop from a healthy individual might be "transplanted" (used as a suppository) into a diseased person, have successfully remediated several diseases, particularly *Clostridium difficile* infection (CDI). A video lecture by Jonathan Eisen at the TEDMED 2012 conference (available at http://www.youtube.com/watch?v=YN1MDwPpch0) offers a good overview of the "cloud of microbes" that inhabits the human body and discusses the science behind fecal transplants.

Going viral

Figure 13. Assessment for proposal to the World Health Organizationto contain H5N1

A. Demonstrates knowledge/conceptual understanding of how H5N1 invades cells. 10 points

B. Drawing depicts accurate representation of H5N1 with clear indication of where intervention is aimed. 10 points

C. Summary of how TAMIFLU acts to combat H5N1 is complete, clearly-written, and accurate. 10 points

D. Drawing (with parts labeled) and accompanying narrative demonstrates precisely how their anti-viral drug will work on H5N1. Discussion of the advantages and disadvantages of the selected design. 10 points

E. Estimate cost and feasibility of your proposal. 10 points

F. INFORMATIVE, LEVEL 3 essay that describes your campaign to eradicate H5N1 globally. Include the following parts:

- How information will be distributed
- Sample brochure or website
- How information will be communicated (not all countries speak English)
- How will other material goods (such as hand sanitizer) be distributed, if at all?
- How will the newly developed anti-viral drug the group developed be distributed worldwide, if at all?
- Where are the disease "hot-spots?" Why are these particular geographic locations "hot-spots?"

See Figure 12 for a rating scale for a Level 3 informative writing assignment.

The proposal should be cost-effective, feasible, and capable of eradicating H5N1. 50 points

Note: The WHO will rate each group based on the quality of information, accuracy of the data, clarity and credibility of the presentation, and probability for success.

SURVIVAL OF THE SMARTEST

INTRODUCTION

The importance of shelter, water, and food to human life is difficult to overstate. Some experts emphasize the "rule of 3" with regard to survival. For example, humans can survive without air for 3 minutes before brain cells begin to die. Humans can survive:

- severe cold for up to 3 hours without shelter (the category "shelter" usually includes appropriate clothing),
- without sleep for up to 3 days,
- without water for up to 3 days, and
- without food for up to 3 weeks.

Albert and Rita Chretien were two Canadians who decided to drive to Las Vegas, Nevada for a trade show from their home in British Columbia. For their trip, they relied upon the Global Positioning Device (GPS) in their van and wound up taking a series of wrong turns, which put them deep into a largely-uninhabited, high desert wilderness of Nevada. After getting their car stuck in a muddy section of road, Albert Chretien decided to walk to the nearest town to find help while his wife Rita decided to stay in the van. After 48 days, Albert still had not returned and Rita was found in the van, barely alive. Unfortunately, her husband Albert was found dead of exposure, more than a year later, about 6 miles from a Nevada town (Canadian Broadcast Corporation News, 2012).

Learning about dangers posed by weather, such as frostbite, hypothermia, heat stroke, heat exhaustion as well as threats from wildlife, impure water, food sources (poisoning), and environmental sources has practical, as well as scientific applications. If students learn the "why" of certain dangers and the "how" of survival, then they can begin to piece together possible solutions through deduction and synthesis. Indeed, because of the multifarious factors involved in a survival simulation, students daily invoke the spectrum of Bloom's taxonomy (Krathwohl, 2002) and Webb's Depth of Knowledge (Hess, 2005).

A unique twist in this survival activity is the inclusion of urban settings. While aspects of the simulation, such as the availability of shelter, water, and food will obviously change in light of the infrastructure of cities, basic human needs and factors of climate and geography will remain cogent. The inclusion of urban settings may help alert students to the challenges of homelessness in large cities. New York City, with a homeless population of 57,000 (Cortes, Henry, De la Cruz, & Brown, 2012), Amsterdam, with a homeless population of 56,000 (Spruijt, Dirks, & Van den Berg, 2012), and Rio de Janiero, with a homeless population of 100,000 or more (Levinson, 2004) represent three of the ten largest urban homeless populations in the world and are the sites of the urban survival simulation.

RESEARCH ON SIMULATION AND PROJECT-BASED LEARNING (PBL)

"The role-playing activity refines students' abilities to conduct research and participate in a debate" and "enhances their ability to speak in public, to present information, and to write effectively" (Oberle, 2004, p. 205).

"When done correctly, cooperative learning has much more to offer biology students than traditional methods. It is hard to imagine why instructors of biology are reluctant to switch to it" (Lord, 2001, p. 36).

"The H-PBL [hybrid project based learning] method may contribute in developing an extended range of scientific and generic skills and may provide a more challenging, motivating and enjoyable approach to education" (Carrio, Larramona, Banos, & Perez, 2011, p. 235).

"Content achievement, enthusiasm and interest among students was, in my judgment, far greater using this approach [simulation] than it had never been in all my experience using the conventional approach" (Stalheim, 1990, p. 485).

RESEARCH SUPPORTING THE USE OF AN INTERDISCIPLINARY
APPROACH TO TEACHING SCIENCE

"Educational research teaches us that it is ineffective to separate learning of facts, concepts, and reasoning because they need to be used together in practice" (Edelson, Wertheim, Schell, & The Leadership Team of the Road Map for Geography Education Project, 2013, p. 4).

"The emphasis should be on scientific concepts, hands-on involvement in learning, interrelations of the disciplines, and their relevance to human life and to the rest of the living and nonliving worlds" (Moore, 1993, p. 785).

"Tying a real world geography assignment to each chapter has helped immensely in understanding the ability of geography to be engaging and not just text driven" (Katz, 2013, p. 28).

COMMENTS ON LEARNING SCIENCE

"Biology and science in general are not considered attractive careers" (Prokop, Prokop, & Tunnicliffe, 2007, p. 39).

"It never seems that any of the students has previously thought about what it means to ask 'why' questions about biology" (Shellberg, 2001, p. 18).

"Educated persons desperately need to recognize, evaluate, and analyze those fundamental premises that give focus to life and give meaning to existence" (Tepaske, 1981, p. 50).

THE LESSON

Survival simulation in six different conditions—desert, dry polar, tropical, ocean, mountain, and city.

ACTIVITY

This activity offers lessons on the human body, geography, climate, and the distinctive flora and fauna of particular regions. Creative, critical thought and sound, scientific thinking are essential to a successful simulation. Flawed thinking will become apparent as students critique each others' plans during the presentation phase.

Students are placed in one of six possible simulations for survival, based upon longitude/latitude.

1. Desert (Sahara, Great Sandy Desert, Great Basin),
2. Dry polar (Antarctica, Arctic Circle),
3. Tropical (Amazon Rain Forest, New Guinea, Central African Republic),
4. Ocean (Atlantic, Pacific, Indian),
5. Mountain (Himalayas, Andes, Rocky Mountains),
6. City (Amsterdam, Rio de Janeiro, New York City).

GLOBAL LOCATIONS FOR SIMULATIONS

Figure 14. Latitude and longitude coordinates of the survival simulations

	A	B	C
1	(25.6, 11.1)	(-20.7, 125.5)	(41.97, -115.75)
2	(-90, 0)	(79.0, -43)	(68.4, -124.4)
3	(-5, -65)	(-5.19, 141.67)	(7.5, 24.0)
4	(28.0, -59.0)	(-7, -125)	(-18, 75)
5	(27.84, 87.0)	(-34.77, -70.29)	(39.12, 106.45
6	(52.37, 4.89)	(22.91, 43.20)	(40.71, 74.01)

Figure 15. Key for the locations of the survival simulations

Condition	A	B	C
1. Desert	Sahara (25.6, 11.1)	Great Sandy Desert (-20.7, 125.5)	Great Basin (41.97, -115.75)
2. Dry polar	Antarctica (-90, 0)	Arctic Circle (Greenland) (79.0, -43)	Northwest Territories (Canada) (68.4, -124.4)
3. Tropical	Amazon rain forest (-5, -65)	New Guinea (-5.19, 141.67)	Central African Republic (7.5, 24.0)
4. Ocean	Atlantic (28.0, -59.0)	Pacific (-7, -125)	Indian (-18, 75)
5. Mountain	Himalayas (27.84, 87.0)	Andes (-34.77, -70.29)	Rocky Mountains (39.12, 106.45)
6. City	Amsterdam (52.37, 4.89)	Rio de Janeiro (22.91, 43.20)	New York City (40.71, 74.01)

ANCHOR POINT

Survival has basic appeal for students from the vantage point of learning useful information about the human body as well as discovering information about climate, plants, and animals in real locations around the world. Thus, the anchor points are primal—survival, the human body, and exercising rational thinking under pressure.

CHALLENGE

The study of longitude, latitude, climate, and geography can become tedious if it is covered only in abstract fashion through memorization. The problem with learning the nomenclature of geography and facts about human biology is that students may forget the information if they have no chance to apply what they have learned. The survival simulation allows students to have a virtual, "lived through" experience that poses minimal risk or deprivation.

TIME

Approximately 8-9 days. Although the survival simulation could be planned over a series of many weeks, making the timeline shorter adds a certain amount of urgency.
Day 1=Introduction
Day 2=Getting oriented, hand out Day 2 tasks, lesson on latitude/longitude
Day 3=Contingency 1: Stay, hand out Day 3 tasks, lesson on climate zones or threats endemic to specific environments
Day 4=Contingency 2: Go, hand out Day 4 tasks, lesson on how to calculate caloric intake and caloric expenditures[1]
Day 5=Learning to survive, hand out Day 5 tasks, lesson on "Why the human body can more readily consume cooked food rather than raw food" or "why water is so necessary for human survival"
Day 6=Rescue, mutiny, or going it alone, hand out Day 6 tasks, lesson on the psychology of survival (rational thinking vs. thought under duress)
Day 7=Students gather materials, lesson=read excerpts from survival stories to give students ideas how to structure the final paper and their presentation. Students may use third person or first person when they write—but the tone and voice should be consistent.
Days 8-9=Students make presentations.

OBJECTIVE

Students will learn about the basic functions of the human body and how the body responds in different environments. Students will learn about geography, climate, flora, and fauna of a particular climatic zone.

SUMMARY

Simulations are commonly used in the training of police, military, surgeons, nurses, and air traffic controllers, where experimentation would be either imprudent or impossible. Baines (2008) asserts that simulation is one of the most powerful instructional strategies available to teachers, only rivaled by direct, actual experience.

MATERIALS

- Several exceptional books and materials related to survival skills are available and included on the resources handout. Provide as much print matter as possible (books, magazines, newspapers) relative to survival.

- Although there are many good websites, quality is widely variable. The *U.S. Army Survival Manual* is available free online at: www.fas.org/irp/doddir/**army**/fm3-05-70.pdf
- One die, preferably an outrageously large, foamy one.
- Provide students with daily tasks and assessment rubrics.
- Bring in the essentials for survival, according to Hawke (2009)—knife (perhaps a plastic version), compass, lighters, and a batter operated flashlight).

SET-UP

Arrange the room for group work (each group has approximately 4 students).

GROUPS

There are four roles in each group: captain, doctor, scientist, and scout. No groups should be larger than 4. For groups smaller than 4, students should divide up the tasks of the missing role. For example, if a group has only 3 members—captain, scientist, and doctor they must divide the responsibilities of the scout among them. A group with only two members must divide the responsibilities of four roles between two persons. For example, the four roles might be transformed into a captain/scout and a scientist/doctor.

CAPTAIN

Understands the problems posed by the situation and crafts an ingenious response. Acts as leader, goal setter, decides whether to go or stay, charts course, decides when and where to travel, assesses severity of threats, decides upon response.

DOCTOR

Addresses potential dangers posed by the environment (heat, cold, disease, insects, physical exhaustion, sleep, injuries from the environment, psychological challenges), formulates responses to those threats, and provides general advice on health and well-being. Tries to keep all members of the group as healthy as possible for as long as possible.

SCIENTIST

Offers data about the environment, geography, climate, poisonous/non-poisonous plants, obtaining water, getting food, typical animals and insects in the area.

THE SCOUT

Responsible for finding campsites, constructing shelter, utilizing tools, making tools from found objects, leading expeditions for food, water, and exploration, helping the captain with navigation.

PROCEDURE

Overview

In general, each student in the group completes one task per day, although the captain is also responsible for communicating with all group members, making decisions, and reporting at the end of each day. After five days, students use drafts to create a single, longer paper that will be assessed for a group grade. Each student also turns in all of their individual work for a grade. The final grade for the project is a blend of individual and group.

1 Week Before Beginning

Tell a story of survival. It would work best if the survival story was local and recent, but a classic survival story (see references) would also work.

Day 1

1. Discuss a recent case of someone who got lost while hiking or while at sea. An Internet search on "survival story lost while hiking" should pull up several stories. Another article about the Chretiens, replete with many photos, is available at: http://www.dailymail.co.uk/news/article-2211532/Albert-Chretien-Remains-Canadian-lost-Nevada-wilderness-miles-town-18-months-later.html
2. Point out the location of the Chretien incident on a map or on the Internet (Google Earth).
3. Ask students to discuss a time when they or someone that they knew were lost. What happened? How did they recover? How long were they lost? Did they have any tools?
4. Have several survival books available for students to view.
5. Tell the story of Shackleton's Endurance excursion to Antarctica. See http://www.pbs.org/wgbh/nova/shackleton/. There are many, many online videos depicting Shakleton's journey. The short version of the story is that the ship *Endurance* was sunk while on the journey, so the crew had to abandon ship. Because there were limited supplies, Shackleton and a five men sailed a small, open boat over 800 miles to Elephant Island, leaving behind the other 22 crew members. Eventually, the boat made it to Elephant Island, but three men stayed at the landing site while Shackleton and two others hiked several miles over snowy, mountainous terrain to the nearest outpost. Eventually, the three men left behind were rescued, as were the 22 men—more than 4 months later. The reason Shackleton and his crew survived was because they knew the terrain, knew how to survive in sub-arctic conditions, and made timely, critical decisions. Students

will be thrust into a survival situation, as well, and the quality of the decisions that they make will influence the likelihood of survival.

6. Hand out "What do you need to survive?" Students rank in importance priorities for a basic (not climate or location specific) survival kit.
7. 3-MINUTE EXPRESSIVE QUICKWRITE, LEVEL 1 Students defend the logic of their choices in writing.
8. Students read their quickwrites aloud.
9. Show and discuss the rankings of Myke Hawke, author of *Hawke's Green Beret Survival Manual* (handout). Some of Hawke's rankings may be controversial, but Hawke's credentials as expert survivalist are unimpeachable.
10. 3-MINUTE EXPRESSIVE QUICKWRITE, LEVEL 1 Students comment on Hawke's suggestions in light of their own. How are they different? Where do they disagree? Why?
10. Students read their quickwrites aloud.
11. Place students into groups of four. Groups of two or three are allowed, but no groups more than four. The roles are: Captain, Doctor, Scientist, and Scout. The captain is the leader and holds a position of responsibility for reporting to the class at the end of each day. You may assign roles or have students select roles for themselves.
12. For the simulation, each group will assume that they have the following: Compass
13. Lighter Battery operated flashlight
14. Knife with six inch blade
15. No food, no water.
16. The group lost at sea will be in an Islander-36 (36 foot boat)
17. Assign groups to one of six simulations first under A, then B, and C as needed.
18. Have students try to find out as much as possible about their location and their new environment. They are lost at this location, without food or water. On Day 2, they will each receive specific assignments related to their new location.

Day 2

1. The teacher teaches a 5-10 minute lesson on how to calculate latitude and longitude. Instantaneous location is available by entering the latitude and longitude coordinates separated by a comma in Google Maps.
2. The captain of each group announces their location on a large map to the rest of class.
3. Hand out assignments for Day 2. Incomplete work must be taken for homework.
4. A few minutes before class is to end, students within the group should report his/her findings to the captain.
5. After hearing all the reports, the captain provides a summary of the group's activities in less than 2 minutes to the entire class.
6. After the captain reports, someone in the group rolls a die to discern the "chance event." The chance event is recorded.

7. Each group, lead by the captain, must take the chance event into consideration for the next day.
8. Tell students that for tomorrow's assignment, the topic will be how to survive by staying in the current location.

Day 3

1. The teacher offers a 5-10 minute lesson on climate zones and discusses potential threats endemic to a specific environment (for example, in the desert, sunstroke, heat exhaustion, thirst, navigation, sandstorms, scorpions, rattlesnakes, and poisonous plants would be threats).
2. The captain of each group announces the chance event and some preliminary ideas for a response.
3. Hand out assignments for Day 3. Incomplete work must be taken for homework.
4. A few minutes before class is to end, students within the group should report his/ her findings to the captain.
5. After hearing all the reports, the captain provides a summary of the group's activities—"the captain's log"--in about a minute to the entire class.
6. After the captain's log, someone in the group rolls a die to discern the "chance event." The chance event is recorded.
7. Each group, lead by the captain, must take the chance event into consideration for the next day.
8. Tell students that for tomorrow's assignment, the topic will be how to survive by navigating to a new location.

Day 4

1. Do a 5-10 minute lesson on how to calculate caloric intake and caloric expenditures. What kinds of foods have more calories and why? How is energy stored in the body?

    Calorie needs based on age (starting age 2), without weight consideration: https:// www.getfit.tn.gov/fitnesstracker/calorie_levels.pdf Vegetable Nutritional Facts:

    http://marshallsplan.com/images/vegetables_nutrition_chart.jpg Misc. Items Calorie Counts:

    http://crescentok.com/staff/jaskew/ISR/chemistry/calories.gif Misc Items Calorie Counts:

    http://www.nzdl.org/gsdl/collect/fnl2.2/ rchives/HASH01b2/93b7bdb5.dir/p027. gif Calorie Burn for Activities based on weight:

    http://drsquat.com/files/pages/zigzag-activities.gif Calorie Burn chart:

http://alldietsource.com/DietPlan/Exercise/Calculator/CalorieBurningChart.pdf

2. The captain of each group announces the chance event and some considerations for his group moving to a new location.
3. Hand out assignments for Day 4. Incomplete work must be taken for homework.
4. A few minutes before class is to end, students within the group should report his/ her findings to the captain.
5. After hearing all the reports, the captain provides a summary of the group's activities—"the captain's log"--in about a minute to the entire class.
6. After the captain's log, someone in the group rolls a die to discern the "chance event." The chance event is recorded.
7. Each group, lead by the captain, must take the chance event into consideration for the next day.
8. Tell students that for tomorrow's assignment, the topic will be secrets of survival.

Day 5

1. Do a 5-10 minute lesson on why the human body can more readily consume cooked food rather than raw food and why water is necessary for human survival.
2. The captain of each group announces the chance event and some considerations for his group moving to a new location.
3. Hand out assignments for Day 5. Incomplete work must be taken for homework.
4. A few minutes before class is to end, students within the group should report his/ her findings to the captain.
5. After hearing all the reports, the captain provides a summary of the group's activities—"the captain's log"--in about a minute to the entire class.
6. After the captain's log, someone in the group rolls a die to discern the "chance event." The chance event is recorded.
7. Each group, lead by the captain, must take the chance event into consideration for the next day.
8. Tell students that for tomorrow's assignment, the topic will be secrets of survival.

Day 6

1. Do a 5-10 minute lesson on the effects of stress (environmental and emotional) on the human mind and body.
2. The captain of each group announces the chance event and some specific strategies that his group will employ to insure survival.

3. Hand out assignments for Day 6. Incomplete work must be taken for homework.
4. A few minutes before class is to end, students within the group should report his/ her findings to the captain.
5. After hearing all the reports, the captain provides a summary of the group's activities—"the captain's log"--in about a minute to the entire class.
6. After the captain's log, someone in the group rolls a die to discern the "chance event." The chance event is recorded.
7. Each group, lead by the captain, must take the chance event into consideration for the next day.
8. Tell students that for tomorrow's assignment, they will work as a group to structure a presentation and a final, group paper. In addition to all previous drafts, they should think of ideas of how to creatively and effectively present their findings.

Day 7

1. Read a 5-10 minute survival story as a model for students.
2. The captain of each group announces the results of the recent chance events and discusses the overall well being of the group.
3. Hand out assignments for Day 7.
4. Groups must prepare final papers and create a creative and effective presentation. Students will turn in their final group papers and individuals with turn in their final assignments on Day 8. Presentation time is 10-15 minutes. Points will be taken off for presentations that are under 10 minutes. Presentations will not be allowed to go beyond 15 minutes.

Day 8 (and 9, if needed)

1. Hand out evaluation sheets to each student. Students also evaluate themselves.
2. Groups make presentations and turn in all papers.
3. After each group presents, allow up to 5 minutes for questions from students. Questions should focus upon the quality of the decision-making in the group under the circumstances.

See handouts for assignments for each group member.

COMMENT

The survival simulation is a way to teach students a rich array of facts, including information about climate, longitude and latitude, geography, human biological response to stress, decision-making, and flora and fauna of the world.

ENRICHMENT

Students may want to create "survival handbooks" based upon their collective work. For extra credit, students may turn their findings into a board game or online survival game.

Figure 16. Five useful survival resources in print

Hawke, M. (2009). *Hawke's Green Beret survival guide*. Philadelphia: Running Press.

Perhaps the most renowned of survival experts, Hawke is well respected among survivalists and military organizations alike. The book is well organized with a plethora of illustrations and examples. The chapter on "psychology of survival" (27) is particularly useful and well worth reading aloud before "Day 1" of the survival simulation. If you are only going to buy one book, this is the one. If you cannot afford to buy Hawke's book or just want to spend nothing, the *U.S. Army Survival Guide* is available free online and is pretty good, though Hawke strongly disagrees with the particulars of some army advice.

Kamler, K. (2005). Surviving the Extremes: What Happens to the Body and Mind at the Limits of Human Endurance. New York, NY: Penguin Books.

M.D. Kamler writes about survival in extreme climates such as the jungle (17), sea (84), desert (124), high altitudes (183), and space (236). Kamler's medical background provides in-depth information on wide-ranging topics, such as pain responses in extreme environments (27), the biological resilience of human hands when injured (32), the biology of mosquito transmitted malaria (35), the jungle disease schistosomiasis (37), the right time to swim in the Amazon to avoid pirhana (39), jungle threats (40-42), the biology of venom (45), treating snakebites (47), deadly caterpillars (49), repelling ticks (54), dealing with quicksand (55-56), using soldier ants as stitches (58), poison frogs (59), obtaining food and water in the Amazon (61), giant edible fish and scorpions (77), responses to lack of air (89-90), the effects of cold water on the body (91), seasickness (92-93), making tools to survive on the water (101-102), the human body's need for carbohydrates (103), the dangers of dehydration (108-109), effects of starvation (112-113), the size of the Sahara desert (125), finding water in the desert (136), the effects of extreme heat (145), the nutritional benefits of dates (148), the body's response to cold (199), freezing to death (200-201), frostbite (229), and hypothermia (233).

Mann, D. & R. Pezzulo. (2012). The U.S. Navy Seal Survival Handbook: Learn the Survival Techniques and Strategies of America's Elite Warriors. New York, NH: Skyhorse.

Mann & Pezzulo combine information on how to survive in the jungle (43), arctic (63), desert (81), and ocean (106) with stories of individuals who actually survived seemingly fatal situations. They include helpful sections on hypothermia (117), water (131), shelter and fire (143), food and hunting (157), and medicine (209). The emphases on climate, finding food and water, threats, and health make the book a particularly useful for completing the writing assignments.

Middleton, N. (2003). *Extremes: Surviving the World's Harshest Environments*. New York, NY: Thomas Dunne Books.

Middleton, a physical geographer and fellow at St. Anne's College, visits Greenland, the Congo, Niger, and Papua. In each environment, Middleton sheds light on how people live in these extremes and valuable information is offered when he talks of his survival or the survival of his guides. In Greenland, he learned to make a shelter (10), how to hydrate (11), how to reheat frozen food (12), ice fish (37), and bird hunt (42). In the Congo, he ate termites and learned how to cook them (63), to avoid ground parasites (81), harvest and drink palm wine (94), create shelter (104), gather food (112), avoid biting ants (113), and avoid jiggers (114). In Niger, he traveled a desert north of the Sahara during which he made discoveries of the roads (166), commented on temperature differences (172), learned proper hydration in comparison to the natives (176), was given proper clothing for desert travel (177), made shelter (179), traversed dangerous sand dunes (184), encountered sand flies and snakes (186), and experienced a desert storm (188). In Papua, he learned that little mosquitoes carry cerebral malaria (194), that a rake is useful in a croc hunt (194), hunted crocs (215), found fresh water (239), and foraged for crickets (251).

Rost, A. (2007). *Survival wisdom & know-how*. New York: Black Dog.

This large book has a nice, large section of advice for traveling on land (261), on the water (317), navigation (387), and the all-important first-aid (425). Under the miscellaneous section, is advice on "ways to improve night vision (461), improvised backpacks (471), improvised containers (473), and "making glues and soap" (473), all useful information for this particular survival scenario.

Figure 17. Additional print resources

Condition	
General	Buchholz, R. (2011). *How to Survive Anything*. Washington, DC: National Geographic Society.
	Kincaid, R. (2002). *Extreme survival handbook*. Boulder, Colorado: Paladin.
1. Desert	Alloway, D. (2000). *Desert survival skills*. Austin, Texas: University of Texas Press.
	Doeden, M. (2012). *Can You Survive the Desert?: An Interactive Survival Adventure*. Mankato, MN: Capstone Press.
	Johnson, M. (2003). *The ultimate desert handbook*. New York: McGraw Hill.
	Middleton, N. (2009). *Deserts: A Very Short Introduction*. Oxford, UK: Oxford Press.
	Nester, T. (2003). *Desert survival tips, tricks, and skills*. Flagstaff, Arizona: Diamond Creek press.
	Piore, A. (2012). Twenty things you didn't know about deserts. *Discover 33*(6): 96.

Figure 17. Continued

2 Arctic	Billington, K. (2008). *House calls by dogsled.* Madeira Park, BC: Harbour Publishing.
	Davies, B. (2013). *SAS mountain and arctic survival.* New York: Skyhorse.
	Hanel, R. (2012). *Can You Survive Antarctica?: An Interactive Survival Adventure.* Mankato, MN: Capstone Press.
	Lansing, A. (1999). *Endurance: Shackleton's incredible voyage.* New York: Basic Books
	Myers, W. (2005). *Antarctica: Journeys to the South Pole.* New York: Scholastic.
	Pezzullo, R., & Mann, D. (2012). *U.S. Navy SEAL guide to mountain and arctic survival secrets.* New York: Skyhorse Publishing.
3. Tropical	Coningham, J. (2003). *Walking the jungle: An adventurer's guide to the Amazon.* Short Hills, New Jersey: Burford Books.
	Doeden, M. (2012). *Can You Survive the Jungle?: An Interactive Survival Adventure.* Mankato, MN: Capstone Press.
	Ghinsberg, Y. (2005). *Jungle: A harrowing true story of survival.* Austin, Texas: Boomerang New Media.
	Millard, C. (2006). *The River of doubt: Theodore Roosevelt's darkest journey.* New York: Anchor.
	Stafford, E. (2011, June 10). My travels: Ed Stafford in the Amazon. *The Guardian.* Retrieved from www.guardian.co.uk/travel/2011/jun/11/ed-stafford-amazon-walk.
	Walden, J. (2001). *Jungle travel & survival.* Guilford, Connecticut: Lyons Press.
4. Ocean	Callahan, S. (1986). *Adrift: 76 days lost at sea.* Boston: Houghton-Mifflin.
	Graham, R. (1991). *Dove.* New York: William Morrow.
	Outen, S. (2011). *A Dip in the Ocean: Rowing Solo Across the Indian.* West Sussex, UK: Summersdale.
	Martin, J. (2002). *Lionheart.* Sydney, Australia: Allen & Unwin.
	Nalepka, J. & Callahan, S. (1993). *Capsized: The true story of four men adrift for 119 days.* New York: Harpercollins.
	O'Driscoll, P. (2005, May 2). Pulled to sea in minutes, teens survive for 6 days. *USA Today.* Retrieved from
	http://usatoday30.usatoday.com/news/nation/2005-05-02-teens-lost-sea_x.htm#

5. Mountain	Daily reporter (2012, October 2). Husband died just six miles from help after he and wife got lost in wild because of GPS ... he died trying to raise alarm but she survived for seven weeks by staying put. The Daily Mail. Retrieved from http://www.dailymail.co.uk/news/article-2211532/Albert-Chretien-Remains-Canadian-lost-Nevada-wilderness-miles-town-18-months-later.html
	Doeden, M. (2012). *Can You Survive the Wilderness?: An Interactive Survival Adventure.* Mankato, MN: Capstone Press.
	Krakauer, J. (1997). *Into thin air.* New York: Villard.
	Ralston, A. (2010). *127 hours.* New York: Atria.
	Simpson, J. (1989). *Touching the void.* New York: Harper & Row.
6. City	Eighner, L. (2002). *Travels with Lizbeth.* New York: Ballantine.
	Gardner, C. (2006). *The pursuit of Happyness.* New York: Amistad.
	Liebow, E. (1995). *Tell them who I am.* New York: Penguin.
	Masters, A. (2007). *Stuart: A life backwards.* New York: Delta.

Figure 18. Resources on obtaining food in the wild

Department of the Army (2003). *Illustrated guide to edible wild plants.* Guilford, CT: Lyons Press.

Smith, H. (1972, May/June). Euell Gibbons: Author of stalking the wild asparagus. Mother Earth News. Retrieved from www.motherearthnews.com/Nature-Community/1972-05-01/The-Plowboy-Interview-Euell-Gibbons.aspx.

Texas A&M University (2013). Common poisonous plants and plant parts. Retrieved from http://aggie-horticulture.tamu.edu/earthkind/landscape/poisonous-plants-resources/common-poisonous-plants-and-plant-parts/.

Thayer, S. (2006). *The forager's harvest: A guide to identifying, harvesting, and preparing edible wild plants.* Birchwood, WI: Forager's Harvest press.

To help with the caloric lesson (day 3), see Frye, B.L., and R.L. Neill. (1987). A Laboratory Exercise in Human Nutrition. *The American Biology Teacher 48(6)*, 370-373. Retrieved from http://www.jstor.org/stable/4448553

SURVIVAL OF THE SMARTEST

Required tasks, by role

Figure 19. Captain

Basic job: Understands the problems posed by the situation and crafts an ingenious response. Acts as leader, goal setter, decides whether to go or stay, charts course, decides when and where to travel, assesses severity of threats, decides upon response.

ASSIGNMENTS

1. INFORMATIVE WRITING, LEVEL 2
Using coordinates for latitude and longitude, place your group on the map (handout). Identify all nearby bodies of water, continents, countries, cities, landmarks and label them. Indicate at least three potential escape routes using dotted lines (- - - - - - -). Label the escape routes by their desirability—1, 2, 3.

2. INFORMATIVE WRITING, LEVEL 2
Contingency plan 1: Stay. If you were going to stay, offer a specific daily schedule. What would need to be done and who would do it? What would you do if someone in the group refused to do their work? How would you regulate eating, sleeping, drinking, and looking for supplies? What about shelter? Should you build a fire? Why or why not? What would you do to attract rescue? Be specific as possible.

3. INFORMATIVE WRITING, LEVEL 2
Contingency plan 2: Go. If you were going to leave the area to find help, offer a specific daily regimen for travel—When will you travel? When will you stop to eat? How will you regulate eating and drinking? How long will you travel each day? Where is your destination? Why there? What will you carry? What will you leave behind? Will all members of the group go or will you leave some members behind? Why? Outline in much detail as you can.

4. PERSUASIVE WRITING, LEVEL 3
Concisely summarize the current situation and explain the viability of contingency plans 1 and 2 above. Which is the better decision? Why? Write a persuasive paper explaining the two options and explaining why your decision, in particular, would be the best for the group. In your paper, persuade all members that your plan would be the best for the group.

5. EXPRESSIVE WRITING, LEVEL 1

Sometimes, the stress of survival situations causes psychological problems and conflict. Write a paper on the psychology of survival, focusing on potential problems and the attitudes of individuals in your group. Who are the weakest individuals? Who are the strongest? Who are most likely to survive? Why? What will you do to insure that individuals maintain a positive attitude? What would you do if one of the two outside members threatens to leave? What would you do if a member says that they should lead—not you? In other words, what would be your philosophy of leadership in this situation?

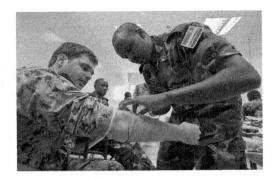

Figure 20. Doctor

Basic job: Addresses potential dangers posed by the environment (heat, cold, disease, insects, physical exhaustion, sleep, injuries from the environment, psychological challenges), formulates responses to those threats, and provides general advice on health and well-being. Tries to keep all members of the group as healthy as possible for as long as possible.

ASSIGNMENTS

1. INFORMATIVE WRITING, LEVEL 2
Provide an in-depth assessment of each individual's health taking into account personal circumstances and the current dilemma. Make a recommendation for minimum daily caloric intake and minimum daily water intake for each person in the group.

2. INFORMATIVE WRITING, LEVEL 2
Assume that the decision has been made to stay in the current location. Create a chart of the biggest threats to health, ideal medical responses to these threats, and how they have to be treated under the current circumstances. For example if you are stranded in the desert, what is the threat of heat stroke and what would be an appropriate response? Would thirst would be a problem? If so, how much water does a human need to survive?

3. INFORMATIVE WRITING, LEVEL 2
Assume that the decision has been made to leave the current location. What additional hazards will traveling pose to the health of individuals? Discuss the top five threats in order of severity of threat (you can provide up to ten if you wish) and the human biological response to each threat. Suggest preventative measures to combat these threats. For example, if snakebite might be a threat, then you might list the kind of poisonous snake, describe how the human body responds to a bite from this kind of snake (is it lethal? What are the side-effects?), and describe how to treat the snakebite to reduce its ill effects.

4. INFORMATIVE WRITING, LEVEL 2
Describe potential biological consequences of consuming poisonous plants, raw insects, or raw animal meat. What happens when a human drinks unclean water?

5. PERSUASIVE WRITING, LEVEL 3
Explain and discuss the risks, benefits and uncertainties of contingency plans 1 and 2 as they involve the health and well-being of each group member. Write a persuasive paper supporting your opinion about the best solution (stay, go, or a third solution that the captain did not consider).

Figure 21. Scientist

Basic job: Offers data about the environment, geography, climate, poisonous/non-poisonous plants, obtaining water, getting food, typical animals and insects in the area.

ASSIGNMENTS:

1. INFORMATIVE WRITING, LEVEL 2
Provide as much data as possible on the environment—temperature, elevation, wind speed, rainfall/snowfall, amount of daylight, any information regarding the location.

2. INFORMATIVE WRITING, LEVEL 2
Assume that you are going to stay. Make a list of ten important animals, insects, plants, reptiles, and other life forms in this environment. Find photos or draw each of them. If it is an animal, reptile, or insect, note its name and habits. If it is a plant, give its binomial nomenclature, and describe relevant information (edible? Availability? Size?).

3. INFORMATIVE WRITING, LEVEL 2
Assume that you are going to go. Describe the terrain, flora and fauna of the area to be traveled. What are some advantages to leaving from a scientific perspective? What are some potential threats? Assess the viability of both of the captain's plans. Has the captain chosen the best plan? Why? If not, what plan would be better? Why?

4. INFORMATIVE WRITING, LEVEL 2
Collaborate with the scout on this question.
Consider the need for food and water. Describe at least ten things that are edible (although some may require cooking). Describe two things that might look safe to consume, but are actually inedible or poisonous.

5. PERSUASIVE WRITING, LEVEL 3
Calculate the amount of food and water against the needs of the group. Confer with the doctor and the captain on the amount of food and water that should be distributed to each individual. Who is most likely to survive this ordeal? Why?

Figure 22. Scout

Basic job: Responsible for finding campsites, constructing shelter, utilizing tools, making tools from found objects, leading expeditions for food, water, and exploration, helping the captain with navigation.

ASSIGNMENTS:

1. INFORMATIVE WRITING, LEVEL 2
Provide an inventory of the materials that could be used to create tools or shelter.

2. INFORMATIVE WRITING, LEVEL 2
Assume you are going to stay. Describe, step-by-step how you would construct a shelter (materials, construction, location, features of the shelter). Provide a drawing and text for each step.

3. INFORMATIVE WRITING, LEVEL 2
Assume that you are going to go. Describe how you would make tools from found objects. What tools would be useful to take on the journey and describe how the tools will be used.

4. INFORMATIVE WRITING, LEVEL 2
Collaborate with the scientist on this question.

If you are on land, answer this: Fire is usually one of the most important aspects of survival. How would you build a fire? What materials would you use? How would you get it started? Provide a step-by-step instructional guide.

If you are on water, answer this: You are assigned to help find food and water. How can you get water from a boat? How can you find food if you are stuck on a boat? Explore some ideas about how to get food and water.

5. PERSUASIVE, LEVEL 3
Consider the challenges and the individuals in the group. Assess the probability of survival for the group. Would survival chances increase or decrease if the group dispersed? Would you prefer to go alone or with the group? Explain.

Figure 23. Chance Events

The rest of the crew (3 individuals) will be selected by choosing three numbers from 1-10. Students should not see this list until **AFTER** they have chosen their numbers.

Figure 15. Three additional members of your party

Individual	Description	Height	Weight
Del	40-year-old accountant, former swimmer, though currently out of shape	5'7"	196
Robert	50-year-old millionaire entrepreneur, former Eagle Scout (Boy Scouts), asthma, diabetes.	6'0"	250
Kimberly	70-year-old mother of three grown children, recently divorced. Former English teacher and social worker.	5'1"	99
Michael	25-year-old college drop-out and chain-cigarette smoker who works as a clerk at a drug store	6'4"	175
Lydia	22-year-old girl who worked in a clothing store. No college. Does not like to sweat.	5'10"	135
MacKenzie	17-year-old high school student with a straight A-average. Runs for the state champion cross country team.	6'1"	145
Taylor	44-year-old account manager for Proctor & Gamble. Sells products to grocery store managers across the United States. Travels 200 days per year, mostly by car, though sometimes by airplane.	5'8"	159
Kim	6-year-old girl separated from both parents. Has shown depression in recent months.	3'6"	50
Rachel	Bright 19-year-old with poor eyesight (corrected by glasses) who was raised by a single father. Won an academic scholarship to college.	5'3"	140
Keisha	Spoiled 12-year-old, picky eater who constantly complains about everything	5'0"	100

SURVIVAL OF THE SMARTEST

Figure 24. Day to day plan

1. Pick three numbers between 1-10. These are each group's three additional members.
2. Each group rolls the dice once at the beginning of the day to determine the chance event.
   1. The extra group member with the lowest number becomes severely ill.
   2. The extra group member with the highest number breaks a leg.
   3. The captain discovers a large animal (you choose the animal—must be indigenous to the environment) that recently has been killed by a predator.
   4. The scout discovers a small animal (you choose the animal—must be indigenous to the environment) that he estimates to have been dead for 24 hours.
   5. An extra group member disappears and cannot be found (up to all three extra group members. If all three extra members disappear, then nothing additional happens).
   6. A huge storm will hit your group in less than an hour (desert=sandstorm, dry polar=blizzard, tropical=very heavy rainfall, ocean=thunderstorm with 30 foot waves, mountain=blizzard, city=icestorm)

Day 1: Introduction
Day 2: Getting oriented

1. Captain=Using coordinates for latitude and longitude, place your group on the map (handout). Identify all nearby bodies of water, continents, countries, cities, landmarks and label them. Indicate at least three potential escape routes using dotted lines (- - - - - - -). Label the escape routes by their desirability—1, 2, 3.
2. Doctor=Provide an in-depth assessment of each individual's health taking into account personal circumstances and the current dilemma. Make a recommendation for minimum daily caloric intake and minimum daily water intake for each person in the group.
3. Scientist= Provide as much data as possible on the environment—temperature, elevation, wind speed, rainfall/snowfall, amount of daylight, any information regarding the location.
4. Scout= Provide an inventory of the materials that could be used to create tools, shelter, or other purposes.
5. Group report in two minutes at the end of class: Your latitude and longitude_____. Show where you are on a map. Explain how you are going to respond to the chance event.

Day 3: Contingency plan 1, Stay.

1. Captain=Offer a specific daily schedule. What would need to be done and who would do it? What would you do if someone in the group refused to do their work? How would you regulate eating, sleeping, drinking, and looking for supplies? What about shelter? Should you build a fire? Why or why not? What is the rescue plan? Be specific as possible.

2. Doctor= Create a chart of the 7 biggest threats to health, ideal medical responses to these threats, and how they have to be treated under the current circumstances. For example if you are stranded in the desert, what is the threat of heat stroke and what should a doctor treat heat stroke? Would thirst would be a problem? If so, how much water does a human need to survive?

3. Scientist= Make a list of ten important animals, insects, plants, reptiles, and other life forms in this environment. Find photos or draw each of them. If it is an animal, reptile, or insect, note its name and habits. If it is a plant, give its binomial nomenclature, and any useful information about it.

4. Scout= Describe, step-by-step how you would construct a shelter (materials, construction, location, features of the shelter). Provide drawings and text for each step.

5. Group report in two minutes at the end of class: Summarize group feelings about staying and update the chance event.

Day 4: Contingency plan 2, Go.

1. Captain= If you were going to leave the area to find help, offer a specific daily regimen for travel—When will you travel? When will you stop to eat? How will you regulate eating and drinking? How long will you travel each day? Where is your destination? Why there? What will you carry? What will you leave behind? Will all members of the group go or will you leave some members behind? Why? Outline in much detail as you can.

2. Doctor= What additional hazards will traveling pose to the health of individuals? Discuss the possible negative impact of traveling on the health of individuals in the group. Write an argument to the captain persuading him/her that either staying or leaving would be best to insure the health of the group.

3. Scientist= Consider the need for food and water as you leave the area to find help. Describe at least ten things that are edible (although some may require cooking) that can be eaten on the journey. Describe two things that might look safe to consume, but are actually inedible or poisonous.

4. Scout= Describe how you would make tools from found objects. Draw the tools and describe how each would be used. Who would be in charge of the tools?

5. Group report in two minutes at the end of class: Summarize group feelings about leaving and update the chance event.

Day 5: Survival skills

1. Captain= Concisely summarize the current situation and explain the most important factors relative to staying or going. Which is the better decision? Why? Write a persuasive paper explaining the two options and explaining why your decision, in particular, would be the best for the group. In your paper, persuade all members of the group that your plan would be the best.
2. Doctor= Describe potential biological consequences of consuming poisonous plants, raw insects, or raw animal meat. What happens when a human drinks unclean water? Provide a list of 5 "foods to avoid" as well as a brief description of what happens in the body when someone drinks tainted water.
3. Scientist=List at least ten things that are edible (specify it items may require cooking). Describe how water can be made safe to drink. Describe how you can make water safe to drink for the group (if you can).
4. Scout=If you are on land, answer this: Fire is usually one of the most important aspects of survival. How would you build a fire? What materials would you use? How would you get it started? Provide a step-by-step instructional guide. If you are on water, answer this: You are assigned to help find food and water. How can you get water? How can you find food if you are stuck on a boat? Explore some ideas about how to get food and water.
5. Group report in two minutes at the end of class: Summarize captain's plan and the group response to the plan. Update chance event.

Day 6: Rescue, mutiny, or going it alone

1. Captain= Sometimes, the stress of survival situations causes psychological problems and conflict. Write a paper on the psychology of survival, focusing on potential problems and the attitudes of individuals in your group. Who are the weakest individuals? Who are the strongest? Who are most likely to survive? Why? What will you do to insure that individuals maintain a positive attitude? What would you do if one of the two outside members threatens to leave? What would you do if a member says that they should lead—not you? In other words, what would be your philosophy of leadership in this situation?
2. Doctor=Write a persuasive paper supporting your opinion about the best solution for the health of the individuals in the group (stay, go, or a third solution that the captain did not consider). This may be in support of the captain's decision or against it.
3. Scientist= Calculate the amount of food and water against the needs of the group. Confer with the doctor and the captain on the amount of food and water that should be distributed to each individual. Who is most likely to survive this ordeal? Why?
4. Scout= Assess the probability of survival for the group. Would survival chances increase or decrease if the group dispersed? Would you prefer to go alone or with the group? Explain.
5. Group report in two minutes at the end of class: Summarize group opinion on

the likelihood of survival and rescue. Update the status of the group. Is the group staying together or splitting apart? Update the chance event.

Day 7: Prepare for the Final Presentation (20 points for each)
_____Quality of decision-making (logical, well-planned, knowledgeable, adaptable)
_____Accuracy of scientific information
_____Quality of writing (vivid description, consistent voice, appropriate vocabulary, grammatical correctness)
_____Persuasiveness of writing (sound evidence, specific examples, good word choice)
_____Quality of presentation=voice (clear, loud, dramatic), props (relevant, plentiful), engaging (fun, interesting), convincing

Days 8-9: Presentations=10-15 minutes for each group
    Read excerpts from any real survival story (see references list). Students may use third person or first person.

The following pieces must be in the presentation as well as in a final, narrative report. Use the previous five days' reports, but edit the various parts so that the report has a consistent, clear tone and voice. Each number below represents at least one paragraph. Each group member reads aloud at least two sections. Props and dramatic presentations are encouraged. The class votes for the 1) best survival plan and 2) best presentation.

1. Explain where you were stranded and describe the surrounding area.
2. Name members of the group (including the three extra group members) and describe each in the context of the current conditions.
3. Describe the surrounding area using pertinent, precise details.
4. Explain the various benefits and disadvantages of staying or going from the place where you were stranded.
5. Explain what was decided and the group response to the decision.
6. What will the group do for shelter?
7. What will the group do for food? Will you cook? How?
8. What will the group do for water?
9. What are the biggest threats to the group?
10. What will the group use for tools? How did you use the tools?
11. What is the group's rescue plan?
12. What happened to the group over the course of the previous five days?
13. What did the group respond to chance events?
14. Why will your group survive?

Figure 25. Survival of the smartest

What should go in a survival kit?

Rank each of the following according to the following scale:

1=essential. Have on your person at all times. You may only select 4 items.

2=urgent. Useful, but not as essential as 1.

3=nice to have. Desirable for a backpack, but not essential or urgent.

_____Beef jerky (pack of two)

_____Blanket

_____Candy bar (pack of two)

_____Canteen

_____Change of clothes

_____Compass

_____Condoms

_____Electrical tape

_____First aid kit

_____Fishing kit

_____Flare

_____Flashlight

_____Gauze

_____Gloves

_____Hammer

_____Hammock

_____Hatchet

_____Iodine

_____Knife

_____Lighter

_____Magnesium bar

_____Magnifying glass

_____Map

_____Metal cup

_____Mirror

_____Net

_____Radio

_____Rifle

_____Safety pins

_____Sewing kit

_____Shovel

_____Soap

_____Sun screen

_____Toilet paper

_____Towel

_____Trash bag

_____Vitamins

_____Water bottle

_____Water purification tablets

_____Waterproof matches

_____Whistle

Figure 26. Survival of the smartest

What should go in a survival kit? ANSWER KEY

According to Hawke, pp. 616-625
Rank each of the following according to the following scale:

1=essential. Have on your person at all times. You may only select 4 items.

2=urgent. Useful, but not as essential as 1.

3=nice to have. Desirable for a backpack, but not essential or urgent.

3 Beef jerky
(pack of two)
3 Blanket
3 Candy bar
(pack of two)
2 Canteen
3 Change of clothes
1 Compass
2 Condoms
3 Electrical tape
3 First aid kit
3 Fishing kit
3 Flare
1 Flashlight
3 Gauze

3 Gloves
3 Hammer
3 Hammock
3 Hatchet
3 Iodine
1 Knife
1 Lighter

2 Magnesium bar
2 Magnifying glass
3 Map
3 Metal cup
3 Mirror
3 Net
3 Radio
3 Rifle

3 Safety pins
2 Sewing kit
3 Shovel
3 Soap
3 Sun screen
3 Toilet paper
3 Towel
3 Trash bag
2 Vitamins
3 Water bottle
3 Water purification tablets
2 Waterproof matches
2 Whistle

SURVIVAL OF THE SMARTEST

Figure 27. Assessment for the survival narrative

Audience: Myke Hawke and a team of professional survivalists

Your narrative will be assessed on how well it addresses your audience (Myke Hawke and expert survivalists). Use each group members' reports to inform the narrative, but edit the various parts so that the report has a consistent, clear tone and voice. Each number below represents at least one paragraph. For the presentation, each group member reads aloud at least two sections. Props and dramatic presentations are encouraged. The class votes for the 1) best survival plan and 2) best presentation.

1. Explain where you were stranded and describe the surrounding area.
2. Name members of the group (including the three extra group members) and describe each in the context of the current conditions.
3. Describe the surrounding area using pertinent, precise details.
4. Explain the various benefits and disadvantages of staying or going from the place where you were stranded.
5. Explain what was decided and the group response to the decision.
6. What will the group do for shelter?
7. What will the group do for food? Will you cook? How?
8. What will the group do for water?
9. What are the biggest threats to the group?
10. What will the group use for tools? How did you use the tools?
11. What is the group's rescue plan?
12. What happened to the group over the course of the previous five days?
13. What did the group respond to chance events?
14. Why will your group survive?

Ideas, 30 points
    Depth and complexity
    Evidence of description, reflection, evaluation
    Good details and examples
Organization, 30 points
    Logical progression or sequence
    Coherence
    Focus
Effectiveness, 30 points
    Sentence structure is varied
    Good word choice

Voice is appropriate to the audience (peers)
Grammar, capitalization, spelling, and punctuation are good
Aesthetics, 10 points
Clear, close-up photographs
Pleasant presentation of information

See figure 11 for a rating scale for a Level 3 narrative writing assignment.

THE PHYSICS OF RUNNING

INTRODUCTION

At one time, runners from the United States performed well in international, long-distance running competitions. In the early 1980s, for example, American Alberto Salazar won the New York City Marathon three times in a row, as well as the Boston Marathon and several 10,000 meter races against some of the fastest runners in the world (Gladwell, 2012). However, in the last twenty years, long-distance running competitions have been dominated by teams from Africa—most notably, Kenya and Ethiopia. Of the top twenty-five fastest times for the 10,000 meters, 13 are now owned by Kenyans; 6 are owned by Ethiopians.

Salazar, who has transitioned from runner to coach over the past twenty years, decided to start an intensive training program, which he dubbed "The Oregon Project," to help train a new generation of long-distance runners. Two of Salazar's students, Mo Farah and Galen Rupp, finished 1-2 in the 10,000 meter run in the 2012 Olympic Games held in London.

How was this breakthrough accomplished?

Although a large part of being a successful long-distance runner is psychological, Salazar used a rigorous, meticulous, scientific approach to help move these elite runners to the new plateau of Olympic champion. Indeed, one of the most rapidly growing areas in sports is the application of science to physical movement, or kinesiology. An indication of the interest in kinesiology is the proliferation of professional organizations associated with the subfield of biomechanics--American College of Sports Medicine,

American Society of Biomechanics, Biophysical Society, Gait and Clinical Movement Analysis Society, Human Factors and Ergonomics Society, International Society of Biomechanics, and the Orthopaedic Research Society. All these professional organizations are concerned with studying the art and science of movement.

The exercises in "physics of running" are relatively simple, as they offer students a grounding in fundamental principles of measurement, a primer on the laws of motion, and a reintroduction to terms that most students think that they already know—speed, velocity, displacement, distance, and friction.

In essence, students learn about one-dimensional kinematics by analyzing their own running or walking. The teacher takes students outside (preferably to a pre-marked athletic field), or to a place indoors (such as a gym) where students can run, measure, and photograph their endeavors. Wheelchair-bound students can participate, as long as their chairs can operate on the running surface. The use of photos as part of the analysis undergirds the practical application of physics and also gives the teacher ample room to extend the lesson to biomechanics, angular momentum, terminal velocity, and a host of other concepts.

For this exercise, a phone (or camera) can be shared by members of the group or each student can use their own. According to the Pew Internet studies (2013), most students (even the poorest students) own a cellular phone or a tablet capable of taking photos.

RESEARCH ON THE IMPORTANCE OF CONCEPTUAL UNDERSTANDING IN PHYSICS

"One of the greatest challenges in teaching physics is helping students achieve a conceptual understanding of Newton's laws" (Kelly, 2011, p. 202).

"We do not want meaningless symbol manipulation; if students use symbolic expressions, we want them to use the symbols with understanding" (Sherin, 2001, p. 479).

"Since we live in an age that makes increasing use of visual representations of all sorts, is not the visual representation a learner constructs a window into his/her understanding of what is or is not being learned?" (Eshach, 2009, p. 589).

"Visualization has been seminal in the development of Western science, and mathematics provides a powerful nonverbal language that allows us to visualize phenomena in the physical universe that we cannot experience directly" (Van der Veen, 2012, p. 365).

RESEARCH ON MOTIVATING STUDENTS TO LEARN PHYSICS

"Physics is often seen by students as hard, and understanding concepts is indeed a difficult process. Teachers often lack strategies to encourage their physics students to undertake the task of seeking understanding" (Unesco

Regional Workshop on the Training of Physics Teachers, 1988, p. 4).

"Many students come into physics with unfavorable views about the nature of learning physics….these views tend to deteriorate after a traditional semester of university physics" (Redish & Steinberg, 1999, p. 28).

"By relating the physics principles to something students have already done, the complex ideas become much more accessible to them" (Creaco, Meyers, & Krauss, 2013, p. 64).

"Students' intuitions about distance, speed, time, and weight are deeply tied to specific measurement units. Students know their weight in pounds, their height in feet and inches, and the speed at which their family car travels in miles per hour. This implies, in terms of meaningful instruction, that it can be beneficial during classroom discussions and scientific investigations for the teacher to strike a reasonable balance between pounds, inches, and miles per hour (customary units) and newtons, centimeters, and meters per second (metric units)" (Sanifer, 2009, p. 9).

COMMENTS ON THE PHYSICS OF RUNNING

"Physics explains everything from the beginning to the end of any complete description of the human body" (Herman, 2008, p. vii).

"Humans sprinting around banked bends change the duration of foot contact to spread the time over which the load is applied, thereby keeping the force on their legs constant" (Usherwood, & Silson, 2005, p. 753). "Each of these body sections has an interdependent relationship with the rest. They each have a 'job' to do and if each one does its job, the machine runs smoothly and efficiently. If one of these parts isn't moving as much as it should, it could inhibit the movement of the others. For example, if you have a stiff neck, it will inhibit the movement of your shoulders, which will reduce your arm swing, which will increase the effort of your legs, which will make your feet work harder than they need to" (Dreyer, 2001, p. 4).

"The velocity profiles for the 100m shows that it took the runner at least half the race to reach top speed, followed by only a slight deceleration in the last 20% of the race. The velocity profiles for the mile and 10,000m show a relatively constant pace through the entire race. However, unlike the other races, the velocity profile for the 400 m shows that maximum speed was reached quite early in race, followed by continuous deceleration" (Reardon, 2013, p. 428).

THE LESSON

Understanding basic concepts in physics through analysis of running or walking

ACTIVITY

Students learn basic concepts of physics through an analysis of students' individual processes of walking and running.

ANCHOR POINT

Students focus upon something of immense interest to them—themselves!

CHALLENGE

Students who are new to physics may feel as if they have been confronted by a universe of strange symbols and ideas. *Physics of Running* provides a foundation for clearing up four common areas of misunderstanding in physics:

1. Unfamiliarity with symbols
2. Different kinds of measures, such as meters per second
3. New concepts, such as displacement and velocity
4. Novel ways of representing reality, such as charts

One of the most consistent complaints about physics is that students fail to see its relevance to everyday life. Physics problems are often misinterpreted by students who are not familiar with the symbols in the problems. *Physics of Running* uses the acts of walking and running to connect symbols with real-life stimuli that students can easily remember.

USEFUL WEBSITES

www.nuffieldfoundation.org
Features information, ideas for experiments, lesson plans, worksheets, and more.
http://www.physicsclassroom.com/
A website mainly authored by Tom Henderson, a high school physics teacher from Glenview, Illinois.

TIMELINE

Day 1=speed
Day 2=velocity
Day 3=momentum

OBJECTIVE

Students will learn how the laws of physics apply in their everyday lives.

MATERIALS

Cones, stopwatch, camera (or phone), 3 handouts (speed, velocity, momentum).

SET-UP

Access to an athletic field, preferably for football or soccer; cleared, grassy area; gym or indoor straightaway. Have ready three cones per group. A class of 30 students would be divided into 10 groups of three. So, 10 groups requires 30 cones. Mark one cone with f, one cone with i, and leave one cone unlabeled. Each group needs a timer and a device to take pictures (such as a cellphone).

PROCEDURE

Day One

1. Ask if anyone has ever run in a race. When? Where? How did they do?
2. The purpose of this lesson is to analyze physical movement through the lens of physics. Coaches of world-class athletes often analyze the form and efficiency of their runners. Although this exercise does not go into biomechanics to any depth, it should provide a framework for understanding the relationship among time, distance, and speed. Also, it emblazons upon students' minds the difference between speed and velocity and the difference between distance and displacement so that they will always remember.
3. Place students into groups of 3 (no more than 4 students per group). If possible, place at least one responsible student per group.
4. Roles will be: particle, timer, photographer. The "particle" is the runner. All students rotate and eventually perform each role.
5. Take students, cones, and phones (cameras) to the location where you have previously marked off 20 yards.
6. Announce to students that they are going to measure their SPEED walking or running. Hand out a SPEED worksheet (see handout) to each student.
7. Place the Xi cone at the Initial location (starting line). Make the point that the i in Xi stands for *initial*. Place the Xf cone at the finish line, 20 yards from the Xi cone. Make the point that the f in Xf stands for *final position*. Encourage students to walk and run in a straight line.
8. One group member walks or runs 20 yards while a second group member times and a third group member records the results on the table. Timers usually stand at the finish line and say, "on your mark, get set, go" pausing after each command and starting the timer immediately after saying "go." The timer stops timing as soon as the torso (chest) of the runner crosses the finish line.
9. The runner records the times in the table and downloads the photos onto the SPEED worksheet.
10. 15-MINUTE EXPRESSIVE WRITING, LEVEL 1 Students return to the

classroom and complete the writing assignment on speed.
11. Students read their responses aloud and discuss results.
12. The teacher highlights correct answers and astute responses and helps students fix incorrect responses or confused concepts.
13. The teacher may want to extend the lesson to include instantaneous velocity, maximum velocity, acceleration, or Newton's three laws of motion.

Day Two

1. Discuss student responses to the speed worksheet and have students report what they wrote in the "thought experiments" about speed. Possible factors in increasing or decreasing speed: stride length, number of strides per second, gravity, slope (uphill, downhill), wind (at runner's back or in the runner's face), temperature (effects of extreme heat or cold on the body), mechanics (arms as pendulums, legs in optimal positions, efficiency of body exertions, i.e. more forward movement than up-and-down movement), gravity (earth vs. moon), oxygen (thinner air at higher elevations), and friction (surface of shoe, running surface).
2. Emphasize that the focus for today's lesson is VELOCITY and DISPLACEMENT, not SPEED and DISTANCE. As in Day one, take students to an area where they can run.
3. For Day two, set the Xf and Xi cones together at the start and set the unmarked cone at the 20 yard mark. Students are to start at Xi, walk 20 yards, run behind the unmarked cone, and return.
4. After all the "particles" have walked and times have been recorded, the next task is running. The photographer takes photos of the runner at the start, middle, and end. The timer captures the elapsed time and tells the time to the runner. The runner records the times in the table and downloads the photos onto the SPEED worksheet.
5. 15-MINUTE, EXPRESSIVE WRITING, LEVEL 1 Students return to the classroom and complete the writing assignment on velocity.
6. Students read their responses aloud and discuss results.
7. The teacher highlights correct answers and astute responses and helps students fix incorrect responses or confused concepts.
8. The teacher may want to discuss instantaneous velocity, acceleration, or Newton's three laws of motion.

Day Three

1. Review the difference between speed and velocity; distance and displacement.
2. EXPRESSIVE WRITING, LEVEL 1

The worksheet on momentum can be completed without going outside. Students can use the time recorded for their first 20-yard jaunt.

3. Students read their responses aloud and discuss results.
4. The teacher highlights correct answers and astute responses and helps students fix incorrect responses or confused concepts.
5. Discuss how momentum can be increased or decreased. Discuss the role of momentum in sports.
6. NARRATIVE WRITING, LEVEL 3
   Ask students to gather all previous writing to tell a story about their experience in their group, measuring strides, timing runs, photographing their form, and computing equations.
7. Go over with students the evaluation rubric for the NARRATIVE WRITING. Offer students an example of a model narrative.

COMMENT

Physics of Running is a fun and engaging introductory physics lesson that should drive home the practicality of knowledge of physics.

ENRICHMENT

The field of kinesiology includes biomechanics (Cerny, 1984) and includes a world of possibility for classroom application in physics. Also, these introductory examples do not account for slope, wind resistance, changes in gravity, mechanical efficiency, or a host of other potential variables. The dexterity of robots has been improved significantly in recent years using kinesthetic prinicples (Wall, 2013; Boston Dynamics, 2013).

PHYSICS OF RUNNING: *SPEED*

Figure 28. Complete the table below. Results in experiments are often presented in terms of meters (length), kilograms (mass), and seconds (time). Also present results in terms that are commonly used in everyday life, such as miles per hour.

A. Name	B. Weight in kilograms	C. Stride length in meters	D. Total number of strides	E. Distance (total length of travel) in meters (approximately =CD)	F. Distance (total length of travel) in yards	G. Run time in seconds	H. Average run speed meters per second	I. Average run velocity (Xf - Xi) meters per second	J. Run speed miles per hour, kilometers per hour
					20				

First, compute stride length before the timed run (from mid-foot to mid-foot). Runner and starter count the number of strides during the race. When the numbers vary, average the two scores. The example moves from right to left, so right to left is the positive direction. Walker/runner stands at Xi. Timer stands at Xf and announces "on your mark, get set, and go" pausing after each command and starting the stopwatch after saying "go." Photographer stands to the side at the 10-yard mark and takes photos of the runner at the start, middle, and end of the race. Place photos of yourself at the start (Xi), in the middle of the run, and at the end of the run (Xf) in the table below. Your results must be confirmed by all members of the group.

| Xf. Finish | Mid-race | Xi. Start |

Xf=finishing position (finish line)   initial position (start line)=Xi

Xf = Finishing position (finish line)

Initial position (start line) = Xi

SPEED WORK

1. Usain Bolt became the 100-meter World Record holder with a time of 9.58 seconds. That translates to an average speed of approximately 23 miles per hour or 37 kilometers per hour. During this particular race, Bolt's top speed momentarily reached 27 miles per hour (43.5 kilometers per hour). Chart the speed of each individual in your group on the graph below. Also, chart Usain Bolt's speed. Place Bolt in the column for 20 yards (though he ran 100 meters).

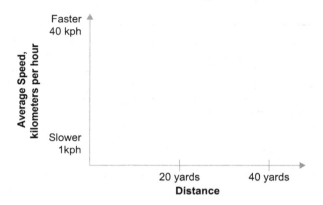

2. Thought experiment

What are some ways to increase speed?

What are some factors that could negatively impact speed?

PHYSICS OF RUNNING: *VELOCITY*

Figure 29. Velocity is different from speed because it is based on displacement, not distance. Velocity is a vector, meaning it has direction (which way?) and magnitude (how much?). Displacement is different from distance. Displacement is measured by calculating Xf – Xi. Xf - Xi is sometimes denoted by ΔX and can be called delta x, or "the change in x." For this assignment, focus on displacement and velocity.

A. Name	B. Weight in kilograms	C. Stride length in meters	D. Total number of strides	E. **Displacement** (Xf - Xi) in meters	F. Distance (total length of travel) in yards	G. Run time in seconds	H. Average run speed meters per second	I. Average run velocity (Xf - Xi) meters per second	J. Run speed miles per hour, kilometers per hour
					40				

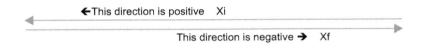

←This direction is positive   Xi

This direction is negative ➔   Xf

The example above moves from right to left (positive), then left to right (negative). Runner stands at Xi. The Xi and Xf cones are both at the start. Place the unlabeled cone at the 20-yard mark. Runners must walk behind the cone (not in front of it). Timer stands at Xf and announces "on your mark, get set, and go" pausing after each command and starting the stopwatch after saying "go." Photographer stands to the side at the 10-yard mark and takes photos of the runner at the start, middle (turnaround), and end of the race. Place photos of yourself at the start (Xi), the turnaround, and at the end of the run (Xf) in the table below.

Xf	Turnaround	Xi

1. Velocity work Your total time for this 40-yard run should be more than 2x your 20-yard run. Why? Fill in the chart with the times of everyone in your group.

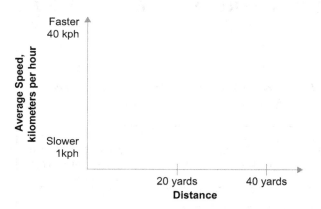

2. Describe how you adjusted your running style to change directions when you ran around the cone. What would have happened if you would have not slowed down to make the change in direction? What happens to cars that do not slow down before making a turn?

3. Thought experiment

In your own words, describe the difference between velocity and speed. In the classic tale of the race between the rabbit and the tortoise, who was faster in terms of average speed? Who was faster in terms of maximum speed? Who had the faster velocity? Explain.

PHYSICS OF RUNNING: *LINEAR MOMENTUM*

Figure 30. Linear momentum is designated by p. Linear momentum (p) is calculated by multiplying mass by velocity. In other words, p (momentum)=mv (mass times velocity).

Name	Weight in kilograms	Distance (total length of travel) in meters	Total distance in yards	Average run speed meters per second	Average run velocity meters per second	Momentum (kilograms per meter/ second)
			20			

Xi

Xf

1. Assume that you gain twenty pounds, but you remain just as fast as you currently are. How will your momentum change? Calculate the difference in terms of kilograms per meter/second.

2. Assume that you decrease your time in the 20-yard sprint by 2 seconds. How will your momentum change? Calculate the difference in terms of kilograms per meter/second.

3. Thought experiment

Professional coaches often film runners to analyze the extent that their heads bob up-and-down while running. In terms of physics, why might a bobbing head slow down a runner?

THE PHYSICS OF RUNNING

Figure 31. Assessment for the physics narrative

Audience: College students, some of whom are interested in becoming faster runners

Organize your writing into the following paragraphs, as described.

_____Paragraphs 1, 2
Describe members of your group
Write about any conversation or comments among group members
Describe first impressions of the assignment

_____Paragraphs 3, 4
Describe what you did the first day (Speed)
Describe the setting
Discuss factors such as the weather, your clothing, and the course
Include as much data on you as possible from the *Physics of Running: Speed* worksheet, including your speed among your group, stride length, and number of strides
Insert photos of yourself in the appropriate places
Describe your conception of speed.
What are some ways to increase speed? What are some factors that negatively impact speed?
Describe thoughts, comments, or events that happened to you and members of your group on this first day

_____Paragraphs 5, 6
Describe what you did the second day (Velocity)
Was anything different about the setting on the second day? If so, what?

Was anything different about the weather, your clothing, or the course? If so, what?

Include as much data on you as possible from the Physics of Running: Velocity worksheet

Insert photos of yourself in the appropriate places

Describe how your running/walking style changed as the result of turning around the cone.

Describe the difference between speed and velocity.

Describe the difference between distance and displacement.

Describe thoughts, comments, or events that happened to you and members of your group on this second day.

_____Paragraph 7

Describe what you did the third day (Momentum)

What are the factors that contribute to momentum?

Consider your style of running or walking. How could you increase or decrease your momentum?

_____Paragraph 8

Summarize your experience dabbling with the physics of running.

Did you learn anything new?

Did anything about the laws of motion surprise you?

What did you learn, if anything, from other members of your group?

_____Paragraph 9

Say you have a friend who wants to increase his/her speed because he/she wants to try out for the 400 meter run at the next Olympics. What suggestions could you offer your friend to increase his/her performance?

Your narrative will be assessed on how well it addresses your audience (students in college, some of whom may be interested in becoming faster runners) as well as how well it explains the physics of running so that they understand.

Ideas, 30 points
  Depth and complexity
  Evidence of description, reflection, evaluation
  Good details and examples
Organization, 30 points
  Logical progression or sequence
  Coherence
  Focus
Effectiveness, 30 points
  Sentence structure is varied

Good word choice
Voice is appropriate to the audience (peers)
Grammar, capitalization, spelling, and punctuation are good
Aesthetics, 10 points
Clear, close-up photographs
Pleasant presentation of information

See figure 11 for a rating scale for a Level 3 Narrative Writing assignment.

THE FIGHT FOR WATER

INTRODUCTION

Since 2007, the state of Texas has filed lawsuits against its neighboring states New Mexico and Oklahoma as well as the country of Mexico in an attempt to divert to Texas some of the water flowing through those areas. In January 2013, despite spending over six million dollars on the lawsuit against Oklahoma, Texas lost its right to Oklahoma's water when the Texas Supreme Court ruled in Oklahoma's favor (Galbraith, 2013).

Texas' quest for water through the courts only highlights the increasing competition for fresh water in the world. As a recent United Nations report on water has noted, "Fresh, potable water is already a precious commodity in many drier parts of the world, and as it grows rare—and thus, dearer—in developed countries, the true value of H_2O is beginning to seep in" (United Nations Development Program, 2012). Since 1900, more than two billion people have been affected by drought (Water.org).

The plain fact is that, as world population grows, access to fresh water declines. Yet, access to fresh water is essential for human life. If nothing is done to insure an adequate supply of water, the United Nations World Water Assessment Programme (2012) predicts potentially disastrous results.

In one possible future, the status quo continues, without further intervention. Growth in food demand resulting from population growth and changes in nutritional habits, combined with increased urbanization, lead to a greatly increased demand for water. Expanding human settlements will encroach on fragile or marginal lands, and there will be increased deforestation and pollution. Climate change is expected to result in decreased water availability in many regions, exacerbating economic polarities between water- rich and water-poor countries, as well as between sectors or regions within countries. Much of the burden of these impacts is likely to fall on the poor. (United National World Water Assessment Programme, 2012, p. 12)

Of all the water in the world, only a small percentage--2.5%--is fresh water. The rest is saline. The relatively small amount of fresh water on the planet is tied up in glaciers (69%) or flows underneath the surface in the form of groundwater (30%). The precious water found in rivers and lakes, called surface water, comprises only 1% of all fresh water.

While most Americans enjoy easy access to water, people in many other countries do not. One in seven people in the world lack access to clean water (Harmon, 2012); one in three people in the world lack access to adequate sanitation resources. "At any given time, half of the world's hospital beds are occupied by patients suffering from a water related disease" (Water.org).

Although water is precious, the average American consumes about 100 gallons of water per day. It takes an incredible amount of water to process food and produce energy. For example, 1,000 gallons of water are needed to produce and process the beef for only one double quarter-pound hamburger at McDonalds (Maxwell & Yates, 2012). Indeed, irrigation for agriculture represents 70% of all water use (Fischetti, 2012).

The extraction of shale gas or fracking requires, on average, 4.4 million of gallons of water per well (Cusick & Colaneri, 2013). Thus, the 35,000 shale gas wells in the United States require the use of 155,000,000,000 gallons of ground water. Of course, fracking contaminates ground water, so the controversy over the drive for cheap energy versus the value of fresh water is a topic of concern in many states.

In the United States and in the countries of the Middle East, in particular, rapid population growth of cities in dry and desert areas poses formidable challenges for the future. The city of Las Vegas, in the United States, recently purchased water rights from several sources far beyond the city limits, some hundreds of miles away. Yet, in Las Vegas, "fully 70 percent of the city's water supply goes toward irrigating the 60-plus golf courses and the many residential lawns in the area" (United Nations Development Program, 2012).

Recent developments in the chemical treatment of water offers hope that supplies of potable water may actually increase for certain populations. The transformation of salt water into fresh water can be accomplished, though the process is energy-intensive and expensive. Portable water purification devices such as Lifestraw, "the slingshot," and the Lifesaver bottle have been recently developed and have made immediate impacts on the availability of potable water in developing countries.

For this exercise, students take on the responsibilities for water management for the city of Las Vegas, Nevada. They must analyze water usage and devise a 10-year plan for water for the city. While the exercise requires knowledge of water science, sources of water, uses of water, and associated costs, the exercise also engages students in thinking about science and technology as they relate to geography, public policy, human rights, business, and the ecosystem.

RESEARCH ON WATER SUPPLY

Close to half of all people in developing countries suffer from a health problem caused by water and sanitation deficits (Hadhazy, 2008).

"Lake Balkal is the oldest and deepest lake in the world. It holds 20 percent of all freshwater in the world. 2/3 of the plants and animals found in its environs are not found anywhere else in the world" (United Nations Development Program, 2012b).

"Projections show that by 2035, 3.6 billion people will be living in areas with water stress or scarcity, as population growth causes more countries and regions to become water scarce" (Population Action International, 2004).

"Advances in health, food security, access to energy, resilient economic growth and climate change all depend on water" (Harmon, 2012, p. 6).

RESEARCH ON WATER DEMAND

International paper used 211 billion gallons of water and discharged 187 billion gallons of wastewater in a single year (Maxwell & Yates, 2012)

"About 90 percent of the Colorado River's water is today diverted into … parched lands for agricultural irrigation. Perhaps half of this regional resource does not even reach the intended crops because it is lost to evaporation and seepage during pumping and transport" (Hadhazy, 2008).

800 million people rely on unimproved water sources (Fischetti, 2012).

"Producing a gallon (3.79 liters) of corn ethanol, for example, consumes 170 gallons (644 liters) of water in total, from irrigation to final processing" (United Nations Development Program, 2012b).

RESEARCH ON USING PERSUASIVE WRITING IN SCIENCE

"To improve secondary students' science-specific argumentative writing skills, and understanding of the content at the same time, the writing students do during school science laboratories needs to be more authentic and educative"

(Sampson, Enderle, Grooms, & Witte, 2013, p. 666).

"Commonly overlooked in studies of Darwin is that he persuaded his peers and the wider community by using plain English words and plain English thoughts" (Kritzer, 2009, p. 42).

"Becoming acquainted with the prevalence of conflict in science is of great importance not only in formal science education but also in the context of informal engagement with science through popularized science depictions" (Scharrer, Britt, Stadtler, & Bromme, 2013, p. 385).

[A demonstration of persuasive writing in action]

"The California Institute for Regenerative Medicine (CIRM) was created by a California ballot initiative to make stem cell research a constitutional right, in response to Bush administration restrictions on stem cell research. The initiative created a taxpayer-funded, multibillion-dollar institution, intended to advance public health by developing cures and treatments for diabetes, cancer, paralysis, and other conditions" (Adelson & Weinberg, 2010, p. 446).

THE LESSON

Students provide an action plan for providing clean and abundant water for Las Vegas, Nevada (or their local area) over the next decade.

ACTIVITY

Using their knowledge of water use and treatment, students map out a plan for obtaining, distributing, and insuring water supply for Vegas for the next decade.

ANCHOR POINT

Students solve a real-life problem facing several cities and towns around the world. There is not one "solution set," as students may provide a variety of tactics to address issues of water security.

CHALLENGE

Many students think that water is endlessly abundant and that all that they need to know about water is contained in the symbol H_2O. The "fight for water" unit requires students to examine the water sources, demand, pollution, purification processes, wastewater treatment, and trajectory for water use in Las Vegas, Nevada for the next ten years.

TIMELINE

Day 1=Current status of water, threats
Day 2=Water purification, wastewater
Days 3-5=Research on water management
Days 6-8=Presentations and debriefing

OBJECTIVE

Students ponder, not only the science behind water purification and wastewater treatment, but get a sense of the intersection of science, technology, public policy, state rights, and the ecosystem.

MATERIALS

Have books, videos, articles, and photos on water readily available for student use.

SET UP

For the first day, show images of the demise of the Aral Sea over time. Also, show images of the area around Las Vegas using GOOGLE EARTH. Consider making large charts of world water supply and demand to put on the walls.

PROCEDURE

Day 1

1. Discuss the centrality of water to human life. More than half of the body is comprised of water and water is essential to human life.
2. Ask students to name as many uses of water as they can think of. Write down all the possible uses.
3. Discuss the case of the Aral Sea. "Aral Sea in central Asia was once the fourth largest body of freshwater on the planet. But by siphoning off waters from the massive lake for irrigation, local farmers and governments in Uzbekistan and Kazakhstan have drained the Aral Sea to 10 percent of its former size" (United Nations Development Program, 2012). As the Aral Sea shrunk, it also became more polluted, which caused fish to die and eventually shut down the fishing industry, which had once flourished around it. In addition to problems with pollution, the saline content of the water increased 400%. An excellent websites that depicts the demise of the Aral Sea is available at: http://www.columbia.edu/~tmt2120/introduction.htm. The Aral Sea has a foundation on the web at http://www.aralsea.org/ and the United Nations has some information and graphics as well at http://www.unep.org/dewa/vitalwater/article115.html.

4. Use the graph available from the free online book from the United Nations: United Nations Environment Programme (UNEP) (2008) to illustrate some of the quandaries about the supply of water and the availability of sanitation, particularly in poor countries. *Vital water graphics.* Geneva: United Nations.

5. 5-MINUTE EXPRESSIVE QUICKWRITE, LEVEL 1

6. After discussing world supply and demand with students, have students venture a guess as to the current state of water usage and supply in the local area.

7. Water providers are required by law (at least, as of this writing) to report to the community the sources and uses of water, as well as the contaminants found in drinking water. Most of these reports are free and can be found online. Encourage students to find this report online and investigate it after class.

Day 2

1. Find the local water report and assess the extent to which student predictions are accurate.

2. The Environmental Protection Agency has a nice list of common contaminants in water at http://water.epa.gov/drink/contaminants/upload/mcl-2.pdf. Ask students to select any 3 of these contaminants, to illustrate each contaminant, to describe its effects, maximum tolerable level, and current status in the local water supply.

3. Have students discuss their findings with the class. Most contaminants could be eradicated from the water supply, so why aren't they? What are the tradeoffs of cost and benefit?

4. 5-MINUTE EXPRESSIVE QUICKWRITE, LEVEL 1

5. Ask students to guess at the process that is used to make local water suitable for drinking. What do water purification processes involve?

6. Have students look up a description of the process in the local water report and to summarize it underneath their predicted process. What surprised students most about the process? Were some students not surprised at all? Why?

7. Describe some of the innovative devices and the underlying principles that underlie the operation of the Lifestraw, "the slingshot," and the Lifesaver bottle. How do these recent innovations work? How does the local water purification process differ from the technology employed in these devices?

COMMENT

The water management simulation is engaging on a variety of levels. Students use their knowledge of water to tackle the urgent, very real problems of water management in the challenging environment of Las Vegas, one of the driest places on earth, where rainfall only totals 4 inches per year (Fishman, 2011).

ENRICHMENT

For teachers who want to address problems of water management on a local level, opportunities for interactions between students and real members of a local water utility or city government would be exciting and educational.

Figure 32. Water Status Report

TWENTY QUESTIONS

1. Current population
2. Description of climate and setting. Include graphs for temperature, rainfall, and snowfall
3. Overview of flora and fauna in the area
4. Population projection for the next ten years
5. Current water usage rate per person
6. Current water usage rate per person compared with three other cities in the United States and five other countries in the world (your choice)
7. Projected changes in water usage rate per person over the next ten years (consider high, middle, low projections)
8. Current list of contaminants, safe levels of contamination, and current levels of contamination
9. Description of current water treatment procedures (drinking water)
10. Recommendations for future water treatment procedures (drinking water)
11. Current methods, frequency, and costs of testing water
12. Projected methods, frequency, and costs of testing water
13. Current and projected costs to purify water (per person and total)
14. Sources of current water supply
15. Current uses of current water supply
16. Projected sources of water supply (additional sources, heavier reliance on current sources, new plans for getting water, conservation, water pipelines, innovative solutions) Wastewater
17. Description of current water treatment procedures (wastewater)
18. Wastewater compared to other cities' wastewater in the United States and with wastewater treatment in three other nations (your choice)
19. Current and projected costs of wastewater treatment (wastewater usage per person and total) Scenarios
20. How might climate change affect your projections? What should be a prescient response to climate change?

Figure 33. Persuasive project proposal

You are the member of a consulting firm that is trying to win a contract to advise the city of Las Vegas (or your local community) on water issues. The name of your firm is

_____.

If your firm is selected for this job, then you will be paid a lot of money and your plan of action will have an immediate, direct impact on the quality of life of citizens in Las Vegas. If your firm is not selected, then you will receive no money for your work and none of your recommendations will be selected.

Audience: Las Vegas City Council (or your local community), which is comprised mostly politicians and civic leaders who may lack any scientific expertise

Purpose: Convince the Las Vegas City Council that your group's plan is the best recommendation for the citizens in the area.

Parts of the proposal

1. Concise, readable, eloquent summary of the "Water Status Report" that includes technical descriptions, but also non-scientific summaries suitable for the audience (City Council)
2. A detailed description of the most pressing issues facing water supply and demand (with your rationale for why the issues you selected are the most crucial)

3. Describe three possible scenarios for water supply and demand over the next ten years:

   1. Probable
   2. Worst case scenario
   3. Best case scenario

4. Recommendations for wastewater treatment and costs Recommendations for water treatment (drinking water) and costs Recommendations for changes in sources of water and costs Recommendations for changes in water policy (demand) and costs Recommendations for any changes or creative solutions

5. Summary of why your overall plan is the best/cost benefit analysis In the written report, include:

   - Cover page with title of the report, firm's name, students' names, and a graphic (or photo) that represents the firm, such as the apple for the Apple Corporation
   - Photos or images that represent your firm's "take" on water in Las Vegas
   - Original slogan for the project (this might also serve as the title to your report)
   - Important points in the text also highlighted in text boxes
   - Photos of all members of the firm in an appendix at the back of the report
   - See figure 10 for a rating scale for a Level 3 persuasive writing assignment.

For the oral, in-class presentation to the (simulated) City Council, consider:

   - Visual, aural, and multisensory props that accentuate the findings and recommendations of the group.
   - Charts or visuals that highlight crucial data or some of your most important points
   - Highly-engaging presentation techniques that will interest your audience and inspire confidence in your firm and your proposal
   - Getting all members of the group to contribute
   - Having at least two persons take on the duties of the oral presentation
   - Not reading the report, but speaking to the City Council members directly
   - Reports should be a minimum of 10 minutes and a maximum of 15 minutes. Presentations will be stopped at 15 minutes regardless of where you may be in the presentation process.

The written portion of the report counts 60%. The presentation counts 40%.

IT'S A DOG'S LIFE

INTRODUCTION

Because there are millions of living things, a system was developed to organize and classify all kinds of life. A man named Linnaeus (also known as Linné) published a book in 1735 called *Systema Naturae* that was only 14 pages long, but it made the case for naming natural phenomena.

In the 18th century, people believed in many superstitions and sometimes they could not distinguish between real and imagined creatures. Thus, in early drafts of his book, Linnaeus included mythical creatures, such as mermaids and dragons, in his taxonomy because people claimed to have seen them. Later, of course, these creatures were found not to be real and were deleted from his taxonomy.

Currently, the most popular system of classification uses a multi-part naming system. The names are usually in Latin and italicized. For example, the name for a grey wolf is *Canis lupus*. *Canis* means dog-like mammal; *lupus* means wolf. The dog is related to the wolf, so is called *Canis lupus familiaris*, or domestic (familiar) relative of the wolf.

As the University of Michigan's Animal Diversity website (2013) explains:

> Every recognized species on earth (at least in theory) is given a two-part scientific name. this system is called "binomial nomenclature." These names are important because they allow people throughout the world to communicate unambiguously about animal species. This works because there are sets of international rules about how to name animals and zoologists try to avoid the same thing more than once, though this does sometimes happen.
> http://animaldiversity.ummz.umich.edu/animal_names/scientific_name/

If you can name living matter, then it is easier for your mind to think about it. If you can get others to agree on the same name for the same thing, then you can identify a specific living matter and discuss it. If everyone called a *dog* by a different name, then it would be difficult to keep track of the different varieties of dogs in the world. Taxonomies help to identify what a dog is and what a dog isn't.

Living matter is classified from broad (animal or plant?) to specific (a particular breed of a dog or a specific plant). However, because the earth has such a diversity of life, some scientists claim that as many as 97% of animals and plants have yet to be discovered (Bryson, 2003). Small life forms, especially, have been difficult to classify—because there are so many different kinds.

It's a dog's life requires students to study, analyze, and categorize animals and plants living in their midst. Through the mechanism of a photo essay, students end up writing an impressive, informative, level 3, research paper.

RESEARCH ON TAXONOMY AND CLASSIFYING LIVING ORGANISMS

"The code has to accommodate a long and bumpy history of often idiosyncratic naming procedures that were unregulated for the first 150 years" (Krell, 2009, p. 278).

"Taxonomy, the science and process of naming living organisms, is a field that is constantly changing. When our scientific understanding of animal species and their relationships changes, it may mean that scientific names change as well" (Myers, Espinosa, Parr, Jones, Hammond, & Dewey, 2012).

"One of the main conclusions from our study is the importance of autoecological knowledge. We see it as the glue between taxonomy and systems ecology. Knowing the names and the often fascinating autoecology can build an interest for learning more about the mechanisms supporting the life in the ecosystem and the relations between populations" (Magntorn & Hellden, 2007, p. 74).

RESEARCH ON USING IMAGES TO TEACH ABOUT TAXONOMY

"Taking photographs enabled participants to contemplate and more readily articulate their thoughts, expressions and experiences about a concept often considered intangible and complex.... Facilitating communication through photos has the potential to provide great insight into lived experiences" (Burke & Evans, 2011, p. 174).

"Capturing and analyzing snapshots of students' real experiences may help ground new knowledge in terms of what they currently know" (Land, Smith, Park, Beabout, & Kim, 2009, p. 65).

"Research in all four areas (attention, comprehension, recall, and intention/ adherence) showed that pictures can, in most instances, provide significant benefits" (Houts, Doak, Doak, & Loscalzo, 2006, p. 189).

COMMENTS ON TAXONOMY

"Overall, tropical rain forests cover only about 6 percent of Earth's surface, but harbor more than half of its animal life and about two-thirds of its flowering plants, and most of this life remains unknown to us because too few researchers spend time in them....at least 99 percent of flowering plants have never been tested for their medicinal properties" (Bryson, 2003, p. 366).

"Even though our rapidly changing world makes the identification of species increasingly important for biodiversity science—and increasingly relevant to the very future of humankind—the field of taxonomy is underfunded and underappreciated" (Drew, 2011, p. 942).

"For the first time in human history, the rate of species extinction may exceed that of species discovery and foretell a mass extinction event" (Wheeler, Knapp, et al., 2012, p. 2).

THE LESSON

Classification of living organisms

ACTIVITY

Students take several photos of living organisms where they live or grow and provide textual explanations of the images.

ANCHOR POINT

The assignment revolves around study of a real, living organism in a student's home or an area near their home.

CHALLENGE

One of the problems of teaching about taxonomy is the binomial naming system, which features 7 levels of classification and a surplus of bizarre words in Latin. As a result, some students may perceive of the task of classifying living organisms as abstract and tedious. To give credence to the importance of biodiversity and the need to classify living organisms, the activity connects to the pulse of students' lives—their pets and their homes.

TIMELINE

2 weeks before due date: Send letter about photo essays to parents.

1 week before due date: Give students the assignment, show them some superb examples of photo essays, give them instruction on the operation of the camera,

approve topics, and tell them the acceptable formats for presentation (notebook, posterboard, slide show, or film).

2–3 days before presentation date: Ask to see students' photographs. Do a demonstration lesson in which you mention aesthetics, page design, and typography. Again, show effective models.

OBJECTIVE

Students will observe and investigate living matter (animal, plant, or insect), and consider the appropriate scientific classifications for the specimen they selected based upon their observations. Students will learn about taxonomy and the Linnaean System for classifying living matter. Students will write observations, explanations, analyses, and predictions.

SUMMARY

The photo essay enables a ground-up, investigative approach to teaching about taxonomy and the classification of living matter. Students choose a pet, insect, or plant that is found in or around their homes and observe and document the interaction of the living matter with its environment. Over half of students have a family pet of some kind—dog, cat, fish, or bird—but if there is no pet at home, the student can choose a plant, flower, or insect instead. Students must generate a great deal of scientific writing to accompany the images that they shoot.

MATERIALS

Students should have access to a digital camera or a device that takes photos (cell phones work well).

SET-UP

Displaying an exemplary photo essay on a bulletin board or in a slide show offers students an expectation for the finished product.

PROCEDURE

1. Send a letter to parents notifying them of your intent to assign photo essays that will likely involve a device capable of taking photos. A cell phone would work well.
2. In class, announce the due date for the photo essay (usually 1-2 weeks)
3. Discuss with students what is meant by the phrase, "A picture is worth 1,000 words."
4. Have several "how-to" books available for students to view.
5. Discuss the relationship between words and pictures in "how-to" books. Many home repair books use a text and photo format as do "how-to" sports books (especially tennis and golf).

6. Show students the Zoobank website (http://zoobank.org/), the University of Michigan Animal Diversity web (http://animaldiversity.ummz.umich.edu/), and the United States Department of Agriculture plant database website (http://plants.usda.gov). Students will use information from these websites for parts of their photo essays.

7. Give an example of classifying an animal.

8. Give an example of classifying a plant.

9. Find living matter over which there is some disagreement as to whether it is a plant or animal. Almost everyone will know about the Venus Flytrap, though most students will already (correctly) think that it is a plant. The classification of a green sea slug (Elysia chlorotica) is more difficult to discern. A short article highlighting some of the confusion over the classification of the green sea slug is available at: http://www.wired.com/wiredscience/2010/01/green-sea-slug/.

10. 3-MINUTE EXPRESSIVE QUICKWRITE, LEVEL 1 Ask students to write about the green sea slug (or Venus Flytrap). Is it an animal or a plant? Why?

11. Students read their responses aloud. Highlight astute observations of students and take the opportunity to correct any misconceptions.

12. Ask students to write out three possible subjects for their photo essays. Potential subjects for essays should be accessible and available for photographs. For example, some students might want to do a photo essay on the cockroach (*Periplaneta Americana),* but it may be difficult for a student to take a series of original photos of a cockroach.

13. Approve or disapprove topics.

14. Show students an excellent finished, photo essay. Several are available through libraries or online. Excellent photo essays on mostly human subjects are available at: http://life.time.com/history/w-eugene-smith-life-magazine-1951-photo-essay-nurse-midwife/#1.

15. Although students will claim that they "already know" how to shoot a photo, spend at least twenty minutes on showing students some fundamentals with regard to cameras—focus, lighting, speed, and especially distance from the subject. Encourage students to shoot close-ups (though they will initially tend to shoot everything from a distance). Before students begin work on their projects, ask to see a photo that demonstrates that they are ready to begin.

16. Do not accept poor photographs.

17. Hand out copies of the *Photo Essay Assignment Sheet* and *Assessment for the Photo Essay* and go over the parts of the assignment.

18. INFORMATIVE WRITING, LEVEL 3.
    Demonstrate how to write text that would accompany each photo in the photo essay. Writing should explain the photograph, but also extend what is readily apparent. Show a sample photo and, soliciting input from students in class, write some accompanying text.

19. Rest assured, you will have to give extensions to some students for terrible photos or for other issues. However, once the students who are behind begin to see others flaunt their photos, they will usually finish quickly.
20. Students present their photo essays in class on posterboard, in a book of photos and captions, in a slide show with accompanying text for each slide, in a film (with a script of the voice-over narration), or on a website.
21. Once students have seen all class presentations, allow them to vote for the best three (see evaluation sheet for more details).

COMMENT

Photo essays are superb artifacts for public viewing, such as open house or demonstrating evidence of student learning. A photo essay such as, "Cutest Canis Lupus Familiaris on Earth," plays well to almost any audience.

ENRICHMENT

The premise of combining image with text has multifarious possibilities. For example, students could create documentation of in-class or out-of-class experiments, replete with explanations, step-by-step instructions and discussion of results.

Figure 34. Geographic Range

Highlight where the animal or plant can be found.

INFORMATIVE, LEVEL 2
Write a summary detailing the range of the animal or plant that correlates to the map.

Figure 35. Classifications

Classification	Human	Lion	Lady bug	Rose	Your choice
Kingdom	Animalia	Animalia	Animalia	Plantae	
Phylum/Division	Chordata	Chordata	Anthopoda	Magnoliaphyta	
Class	Mammalia	Mammalia	Insecta	Magnoliopsida	
Order	Primate	Carnivora	Coleoptera	Rosales	
Family	Homindae	Felidae	Coccinellidae	Rosaceae	
Genus	Homo	Panthera	Hippodamia	Rosoideae	
Species	sapiens	leo	convergens	rosa	

Figure 36. Photo Essay Assignment Sheet--ANIMAL

IT'S A DOG'S LIFE

Informative Writing, Level 3

You must write accompanying text for every photo.

Original photos and text
At least 2 original photos of the habitat with text describing the animal's home
At least 2 original photos depicting the appearance of the animal with text describing how the animal looks and acts
At least 2 original photos depicting typical behavior with text describing some typical behaviors.
At least 2 original photos of the animal with text describing how well the animal sees and hears as well as how the animal communicates.
At least 1 original photo showing the animal eating along with text describing food habits. What does the animal eat?
At least 1 original photo or drawing depicting the animal's role in the ecosystem and its relationship with humans.

_____total of at least 10 original photos

Borrowed photos and text
Some images may be difficult to get, so you can use images from books, magazines, or the Internet. Make sure that you identify where you found the image you are using. For example, you might write, "Image retrieved from http://bugguide.net/node/view/179896" if you borrowed an image from the bugguide.

At least one image representing reproduction with text that answers these questions
Eggs or live babies?
How many babies are born at one time?
How long does pregnancy last?
At least two images representing lifespan.
One image of a young animal with description of features of the young
One image of an old animal with description of features of the old
How long does the animal live?
At least one image of a predator
Find at least one image of an enemy and describe the animal's enemies.
At least one image of prey
Find at least one image of potential prey and describe the animals that your animal preys upon.

_____At least 5 additional photos (either your original photo or from another sources)

Figure 37. Photo Essay Assignment Sheet--PLANT

IT'S A DOG'S LIFE

Informative Writing, Level 3

You must write accompanying text for every photo.

Original photos and text
At least 2 original photos of the kinds of places where the plant can be found.
At least 2 original photos highlighting specific characteristics of the plant.
At least 1 original photo describing the uses of the plant.
At least 1 original photo describing how the current status of the plant (is it prolific or endangered?)
At least 1 original photo describing how make the plant flourish or to help the plant get established.
At least 1 original photo describing how the plant responds to darkness.
At least 1 original photo that shows how to detect when the plant is suffering.
At least 1 original photo or drawing that depicts the plant's role in the ecosystem and its relationship with humans.

_____total of at least 10 original photos

Borrowed photos and text
Some images may be difficult to get, so you can use images from books, magazines, or the Internet. Make sure that you identify where you found the image you are using. For example, you might write, "Image retrieved from http://plants.usda.gov/java/" if you borrowed an image from the National Resource Conservation Service website.

At least one image representing plant reproduction with text that answers these questions
How does the plant reproduce?
How does the plant get distributed? (pollination, wind, self-fertilization?)
At least one image of a seed
Describe ideal growing conditions
At least two images representing life span
One image of a young plant with description of features
One image of an old plant with description of features
How long does the plant live?
At least one image of a pest or potential threats
Find at least one image of a pest and describe some potential threats.
_____At least 5 additional photos (either your original photo or from another sources)

Figure 38. Assessment for the biodiversity photo essay

IT'S A DOG'S LIFE

_____Minimum of 15 photos (20 points)

_____Photos are in focus, well-lighted, good contrast, sufficiently close-up, and relevant to the topic. (20 points)

_____Information is clearly written and easy to understand. Text uses precise and appropriate language. Text describes the photos, but also extends the message beyond the photos. (20 points)

_____Map of where the animal/plant/insect lives is neat and correct. Classification of animal or plant is correct. (20 points)

_____Aesthetics (presentation of text and photos) (20 points)

See figure 12 for a rating scale for a Level 3 informative writing assignment.

Comments:

REFERENCES

CHAPTER 1

College Board. (2004). *Writing: A ticket to work or a ticket out?* New York, NY: The College Board.

Craven, G. (2009). *What's the worst that could happen?* New York, NY: Perigee.

Day, S. P., & Bryce, T. K. (2013). The benefits of cooperative learning to socio-scientific discussion in secondary school science. *International Journal Of Science Education, 35*(9), 1533–1560.

Ebizmba. (2013). *Most popular science sites.* Retrieved from http://www.ebizmba.com/articles/science-websites

Farr, R. (2013). *What kids are reading.* Wisconsin Rapids, WI: Renaissance Learning.

Farrington, C. A., Roderick, M., Allensworth, E., Nagaoka, J., Keyes, T. S., Johnson, D. W., & Beechum, N. O. (2012). *Teaching adolescents to become learners. The role of noncognitive factors in shaping school performance: A critical literature review.* Chicago, IL: University of Chicago Consortium on Chicago School Research.

Hillocks, G. (1986). *Research on written composition.* Urbana, IL: National Council of Teachers of English.

Hillocks, G. (1999). *Ways of thinking, ways of teaching.* New York, NY: Teachers College Press.

Knickerbocker, B. (2007, December 20). A rural teacher with global reach. *Christian Science Monitor.* Retrieved from http://www.csmonitor.com/2007/1220/p13s04-legn.html

National Assessment of Educational Progress. (2010). *Writing framework for the 2011 National Assessment of Educational Progress.* Washington, DC: U.S. Government Printing Office.

National Assessment of Educational Progress. (2008). *Reading framework for the 2009 National Assessment of Educational Progress.* Washington, DC: U.S. Government Printing Office.

National Assessment of Educational Progress. (2000a). NAEP Scoring of Eighth-Grade Informative Writing, *NAEP Facts, 5*(2), 3.

National Assessment of Educational Progress. (2000b). NAEP Scoring of Twelfth-Grade Persuasive Writing, *NAEP Facts, 5*(3), 3.

National Archives. (2013). *Letter from Albert Einstein to President Franklin D. Roosevelt, 08/02/1939.* Retrieved from http://research.archives.gov/description/593374

OECD. (2012). *OECD Science, technology and industry outlook 2012.* Retrieved from OCED Publishing: http://dx.doi.org/10/1787/sti_outlook-2012-en

Stinner, A., & Metz, D. (2004). Using thought experiments to teach Einstein's ideas. *Fifth International Conference for history of Science in Science Education,* 133–144. Retrieved from http://sci-ed.org/conferences/proceedings/proceedings-of-the-fifth-international-conference-for-history-of-science-in-science-education/

Stormer, K. (2013). *Why can't Tyrone write?* (Unpublished doctoral dissertation). The University of Oklahoma.

Topping, K. J., Thurston, A. A., Tolmie, A. A., Christie, D. D., Murray, P. P., & Karagiannidou, E. E. (2011). Cooperative learning in science: intervention in the secondary school. *Research In Science & Technological Education, 29*(1), 91–106.

WolframAlpha. (2014). *Site for educators.* Retrieved from http://education.wolfram.com

Youtube (2013). Statistics. Retrieved from http://www.youtube.com/yt/press/statistics.html.

CHAPTER 2

ACT. (2007). *Writing Specifications for the 2011 National Assessment of Educational Progress.* Iowa City, IA: ACT.

Francek, M. (2013). A compilation and review of over 500 geoscience misconceptions. *International Journal of Science Education, 35*(1), 31–64.

REFERENCES

Heddy, B. C., & Sinatra, G. M. (2013). Transforming misconceptions: Using transformative experience to promote positive affect and conceptual change in students learning about biological evolution. *Science Education, 97*(5), 723–744.

Hillocks, G. (2011). *Teaching Argument Writing, Grades 6-12: Supporting Claims with Relevant Evidence and Clear Reasoning*. Portsmouth, NH: Heinemann.

Hillocks, G. (1986). *Research on written composition*. Urbana, IL: National Council of Teachers of English.

National Assessment Governing Board. (2010). *NAEP 2011 Writing Frameworks*. Washington DC: U.S. Government Printing Office.

National Center for Education Statistics. (1999). *NAEP 1996 trends in writing: Fluency and writing conventions*. Washington, DC: U.S. Department of Education.

National Center for Education Statistics. (2000). Focused holistic scoring. *NAEP Facts, 5*(3).

Stedman, L. (2009). *The NAEP long-term trend assessment: A review of its transformation, use, and findings*. Washington, DC: National Assessment Governing Board (NAGB).

CHAPTER 3

Borody, T. J., & Khoruts, A. (2012). Fecal microbiota transplantation and emerging applications. *Nature Reviews Gastroenterology and Hepatology, 9*, 88–96.

Cantor Arts Center. (2013). *Adventures in the human virosphere: The use of three-dimensional models to understand human viral infections*. Retrieved from http://museum.stanford.edu/news_room/virosphere.html

Beltran, W., Cideciyan, A., Lewin, A., Iwabe, S; Khanna, H., Sumaroka, A., Chiodo, V.,…Aguirre, G. (2012). Gene therapy rescues photoreceptor blindness in dogs and paves the way for treating human X-linked retinitis pigmentosa. *Proceedings of the National Academy of Sciences USA, 109*(6), 2132–2137.

Blankinship, L. A. (2011). Teaching bacterial arrangements and morphologies with candy. *Journal of Microbiology & Biology Education, 12*(1), 69–70.

Burleson, K. M., & Martinez-Vaz, B. M. (2011). Microbes in mascara: Hypothesis-driven research in a nonmajor biology lab. *Journal of Microbiology & Biology Education, 12*(2), 166–175.

Cepko,C., & Vandenberghe L. (2013). Retinal gene therapy coming of age. *Human Gene Therapy, 24*(3), 242–244.

Cherif, A. H., Siuda, J. E., & Movahedzadeh, F. (2013). Developing nontraditional biology labs to challenge students & enhance learning. *The American Biology Teacher, 75*(1), 14–17.

Dolberry, A. A. (2010). The sci-Fi microbe: Reinforcing understanding of microbial structures and their significance through a creative writing exercise. *Journal of Microbiology & Biology Education, 11*(2), 175–176.

Dunn, R. (2011, July 5). *Scientists discover that antimicrobial wipes and soaps may be making you (and society) sick. Scientific American*. Retrieved from http://blogs.scientificamerican.com/guest-blog/2011/07/05/scientists-discover-that-antimicrobial-wipes-and-soaps-may-be-making-you-and-society-sick/

Fischbach, M., Bluestone, J., & Lim, W. (2013). Cell-based therapeutics: The next pillar of medicine. *Science Translational Medicine, 5*(179). Retrieved from http://stm.sciencemag.org/content/5/179/179ps7.full

Gevers, D., Knight, R., Petrosinio, J. F., Huang, K., McGuire, A. L., Birren, B. W.,…Huttenhower, C. (2012). The human microbiome project: A community resource for the healthy human microbiome. *PLOS Biology, 10*(8).

Goodsell, D. S. (2012). Illustrating the machinery of life: Viruses. *Biochemistry and Molecular Biology Education, 40*(5), 291–296.

Hylton, W. S. (2012, May 30). Craig Venter's bugs might save the world. *The New York Times*. Retrieved from http://www.nytimes.com/2012/06/03/magazine/craig-venters-bugs-might-save-the-world.html?pagewanted=all&_r=0

Kolata, G. (2012, June 14). In good health? Thank your 100 trillion bacteria. *The New York Times*. Retrieved from http://www.nytimes.com/2012/06/14/health/human-microbiome-project-decodes-our-100-trillion-good-bacteria.html?pagewanted=all

Kuniyuki, A., & G. Sharp (2011). Designing cancer-killing viruses to improve student understanding of microbiology. *Journal of Microbiology & Biology Education, 12*(2), 135–142.

Lewis, C. M. Jr., Obregón-Tito, A., Tito, R. Y., Foster, M. W., & Spicer, P. G. (2012). The human microbiome project: Lessons from human genomics. *Trends in Microbiology, 20*(1), 1–4.

MacIver, M. (2011, December 27). Information wants to be free. What about killer information? *Discover Magazine*. Retrieved from http://blogs.discovermagazine.com/crux/2011/12/27/information-wants-to-be-free-what-about-killer-information/#.UcICOIWfsQU

National Institutes of Health Human Microbiome Project. (2013). *About HMP metagenomic sequencing and analysis*. Retrieved from http://www.hmpdacc.org/micro_analysis/microbiome_analyses.php

Reynolds, J. A., Thaiss, C., Katkin, W., & Thompson, R. J. Jr. (2012). Writing-to-Learn in undergraduate science education: A community-based, conceptually driven approach. *CBE-Life Sciences Education, 11*, 17–25.

Shors, T. (2013). *Understanding viruses*. Burlington, MA: Jones & Barlett.

Turnbaugh, P. J., Ley, R. E., Hamady, M., Fraser-Liggett, C. M., Knight, R., & Gordon, J. I. (2007). The human microbiome project. *Nature International Weekly Journal of Science, 449*, 804–810.

Walsh, F. (2012, April 2). H5N1 bird blu research to be published in full. *BBC News*. Retrieved from http://www.bbc.co.uk/news/health-17585328

World Health Organization. (2013). *H5N1 research issues*. Retrieved from http://www.who.int/influenza/human_animal_interface/avian_influenza/h5n1_research/en/index.html

Zimmer, C. (2012, June 18). Tending the Body's Microbial Garden. *The New York Times*. Retrieved from http://www.nytimes.com/2012/06/19/science/studies-of-human-microbiome-yield-new-insights.html?pagewanted=all

CHAPTER 4

Baines, L. (2008). *A teacher's guide to multisensory learning*. Alexandria, VA: ASCD.

Boston Dynamics. (2013). *Changing your idea of what a robot can do*. Retrieved from http://www.bostondynamics.com/index.html

Canadian Broadcast Corporation News. (2012, October 1). *Body of missing B.C. man albert Chreitien found in Nevada*. Retrieved from http://www.cbc.ca/news/canada/british-columbia/story/2012/10/01/albert-chretien-body-found.html

Carrió, M., Larramona, P., Baños, J. E., & Pérez, J. (2011). The effectiveness of the hybrid problem-based learning approach in the teaching of biology: A comparison with lecture-based learning. *Journal of Biological Education, 45*(4), 229–235. Retrieved from http://dx.doi.org/10.1080/00219266.2010.546011

Cortes, A., Henry, M., De la Cruz, R., & Brown, S. (2012). *The 2012 point-in-time estimates of homelessness*. Washington, DC: The U.S. Department of Housing and Urban Development Office of Community Planning and Development.

Edelson, D. C., Wertheim, J. A., Schell, E. M., & The Leadership Team of the Road Map for Geography Education Project. (2013). Creating a Road Map for 21st Century Geography Education: Project Overview. *The Geography Teacher, 10*(1), 1–5. Retrieved from http://dx.doi.org/10.1080/19338341.2012.758045

Hess, K. (2005). *Applying Webb's Depth-of-Knowledge (DOK) Levels in writing*. Retrieved from http://www.nciea.org/publications/DOKwriting_KH08.pdf

Katz, R. (2013). Using "Petites Projects" to further engage students in Geography. *The Geography Teacher, 10*(1), 28–33. doi: http://dx.doi.org/10.1080/19338341.2012.758042.

Krathwohl, D. (2002). A revision of Bloom's Taxonomy: An overview. *Theory into Practice, 41*(4), 212–218.

Levinson, D. (2004). *Encyclopedia of homelessness*. Thousand Oaks, CA: Sage.

REFERENCES

Lord, T. R. (2001). 101 reasons for using cooperative learning in biology teaching. *The American Biology Teacher, 63*(1), 30–38.
Moore, J. A. (1993). We need a revolution—teaching biology for the twenty-first century. *Bioscience, 43*(11), 782–786.
Oberle, A. P. (2004). Understanding public land management through role-playing. *Journal of Geography, 103*(5), 199–210.
Prokop, P., Prokop, M., & Tunnicliffe, S. (2007). Is biology boring? Student attitudes toward biology. *Journal of Biological Education, 42*(1), 36–39.
Shellberg, T. (2001). Teaching how to answer 'why' questions about biology. *The American Biology Teacher, 63*(1), 16–19.
Spruijt, J., Dirks, D., & Van den Berg, D. (2012). *Social exclusion of homeless people in The Netherlands.* Retrieved from netaware.ue.katowice.pl/.../Social-exclusion-of-homeless-people-in-The-Netherlands.
Stalheim, B. (1990). Staying alive: Problems of survival. *The American Biology Teacher, 52*(8), 484–486. Retrieved from http://www.jstor.org/stable/4449181
Tepaske, E. R. (1981). Teaching about survival: Some hidden assumptions. *The American Biology Teacher, 43*(1). Retrieved from http://www.jstor.org/stable/4447114

CHAPTER 5

Borody, T. J. & Khoruts, A. (2012). Fecal microbiota transplantation and emerging applications, *Nature Reviews Gastroenterology and Hepatology, 9,* 88–96.
Cerny, K. (1984). Kinesiology vs. biomechanics. *Physical Therapy, 64*(12), 1809.
Creaco, A., Meyers, W., & Krauss, D. (2013). Applying Newton's third law of motion in the gravitron ride. *Journal of College Science Teaching, 42*(4), 64–67.
Dreyer, D. (2001, May 1). Physical running. *Runner's world.* Retrieved from http://www.runnersworld.com/race-training/physical-running?page=single.
Eshach, H. (2009). Using photographs to probe students' understanding of physical concepts: The case of Newton's 3rd law. *Research in science education, 40,* 589–603.
Gladwell, M. (2012, July 30). Alberto Salazar and the art of exhaustion. *New Yorker,* 26–29.
Herman, I. (2008). *Physics of the human body.* New York, NY: Springer.
Kelly, A. (2011, April). Teaching Newton's laws with the iPod Touch in conceptual physics. *The Physics Teacher, 49,* 202–205.
Nuffield Foundation. (2013). *Website.* Retrieved from www.nuffieldfoundation.org
Pew Research. (2013). *Teens and Technology.* Washington, DC: Pew Research Center. Retrieved from http://www.pewinternet.org/Reports/2013/Teens-and-Tech.aspx
The Physics Classroom. (2013). *Website.* Retrieved from http://www.physicsclassroom.com
Reardon, J. (2013). Optimal pacing for running 400- and 800-m track races. *American Journal of Physics, 81*(6), 428–436.
Redish, E., & Steinberg, R. (1999). Teaching physics: Figuring out what works. *Physics Today, 52,* 24–30.
Sandifer, C. (2009, May/June). Tips for teachers. *Connect,* 8–10.
Sherin, B. (2001). How students understand physics equations. *Cognition and instruction, 19*(4), 479–541.
Unesco Regional Workshop on the Training of Physics Teachers (1988). *A fresh look at teaching physics at school level.* Bangkok: United Nations Educational, Scientific and Cultural Organization.
Usherwood, J., & Silson, A. (2005, December). No force limit on greyhound sprint speed. *Nature, 438*(8), 753–754.
Van der Veen, J. (2012). Draw your physics homework? Art as a path to understanding in physics teaching. *American Educational Research Journal, 49,* 356–407.
Wall, M. (2013, October 7). Pentagon-funded Atlas robot refuses to be knocked over. *BBC News.* Retrieved from http://www.bbc.co.uk/news/technology-24427821

CHAPTER 6

Adelson, J. W., & Weinberg, J. K. (2010). The California stem cell initiative: Persuasion, politics, and public science. *American Journal Of Public Health, 100*(3), 446–451.

Cusick, M., & Colaneri, K. (2013). *How much water does it take to frack a well? Stateimpact Pennsylvania.* Retrieved from http://stateimpact.npr.org/pennsylvania/2013/03/12/how-much-water-it-takes-to-frack-a-well/

Environmental Protection Agency. (2013). *Watersense: Indoor water use in the United States.* Retrieved from www.epa.gov/WaterSense/pubs/indoor.html

Fischetti, M. (2012, May 21). How much water do nations consume? *Scientific American.* Retrieved from http://www.scientificamerican.com/article.cfm?id=graphic-science-how-much-water-nations-consume

Fishman, C. (2011). *The big thirst.* New York, NY: Free Press.

Galbraith, K. (2013, June 13). *Supreme court backs Oklahoma over Texas water district. Texas Tribute.* Retrieved from http://www.texastribune.org/2013/06/13/supreme-court-decides-texas-oklahoma-water-case/

Hadhazy, A. (2008, July 23). Top ten water wasters. *Scientific American.* Retrieved from www.scientificamerican.com/article.cfm?id=top-10-water-wasters

Harmon, K (2012). Improved but not always safe: Despite global efforts, more than 1 billion people likely at risk for lack of clean water. *Scientific American.* Retrieved from www.scientificamerican.com/article/cfm?id=improved-but-not-always-safe

Kritzer, H. M. (2009). The arts Of persuasion in science and law: Conflicting norms in the courtroom. *Law & Contemporary Problems, 72*(1), 41–61.

Maxwell, S., & Yates, S. (2012). *The future of water.* Denver, CO: American Water Works Association.

Population Action International. (2004). *People in the Balance Update 2004: Population and Natural Resources at the Turn of the Millennium.* Washington, DC: PAI. Retrieved from http://populationaction.org/wp-content/uploads/2012/04/PAI-1293-WATER-4PG.pdf

Sampson, V., Enderle, P., Grooms, J., & Witte, S. (2013). Writing to learn by learning to write during the school science laboratory: Helping middle and high school students develop argumentative writing skills as they learn core ideas. *Science Education, 97*(5), 643–670.

Scharrer, L., Britt, M., Stadtler, M., & Bromme, R. (2013). Easy to understand but difficult to decide: Information comprehensibility and controversiality affect laypeople's science-based decisions. *Discourse Processes, 50*(6), 361–387.

United Nations World Water Development Programme. (2012a). *Managing water under uncertainty and risk.* Geneva, Switzerland: United Nations Publishing.

United Nations Development Program. (2012b). *Every drop matters.* Retrieved from www.everydropmatters.com

Water.org. (2013). *Global water crisis basic facts sheet.* Retrieved from www.water.org

Watersense: Indoor water use in the United States. Retrieved from www.epa.gov/WaterSense/pubs/indoor.html

CHAPTER 7

Bryson, B. (2003). *A short history of nearly everything.* New York, NY: Broadway Books.

Burke, D., & Evans, J. (2011). Embracing the creative: The role of photo Novella in qualitative nursing research. *International Journal Of Qualitative Methods, 10*(2), 164–177.

Drew, L. (2011, December). Are we losing the science of taxonomy? *Bioscience, 61*(12), 942–946.

Houts, P., Doak, C., Doak, L., & Loscalzo, M. (2006). The role of pictures in improving health communication. *Patient Education and Counseling, 61,* 173–190.

Krell, F. (2009). ZooBank and the next edition of the Code—challenges and new developments in the 250th year of zoological nomenclature, *Aquatic Insects, 31* (supplement 1), 269–282.

Land, S., Smith, B., Park, S., Beabout, B., & Kim, K. (2009). Supporting school-home connections through photo journaling: Capturing everyday experiences of nutrition concepts. *Techtrends: Linking Research & Practice To Improve Learning, 53*(6), 61–65.

REFERENCES

Magntorn, O., & Hellden, G. (2007, spring). Reading nature from a 'bottom up' perspective. *Journal of Biological Education, 41*(2), 68–75.

Myers, P., Espinosa, R., Parr, C. S., Jones, T., Hammond, G. S., & Dewey, T. S. (2012). *The animal diversity web (online)*. Retrieved from http:/animaldiversity.org

University of Michigan Animal Diversity Website. (2013). *What is in a scientific name?* Retrieved from http://animaldiversity.ummz.umich.edu/animal_names/scientific_name/

Wheeler, Q., Knapp, S., Stevenson, D., Stevenson, J., Blum, S., Boom, B.,...Woolley J. (2012). Mapping the biosphere: exploring species to understand the origin, organization and sustainability of biodiversity, *Systematics and Biodiversity, 10*(1), 1–20.

Printed in the United States
By Bookmasters